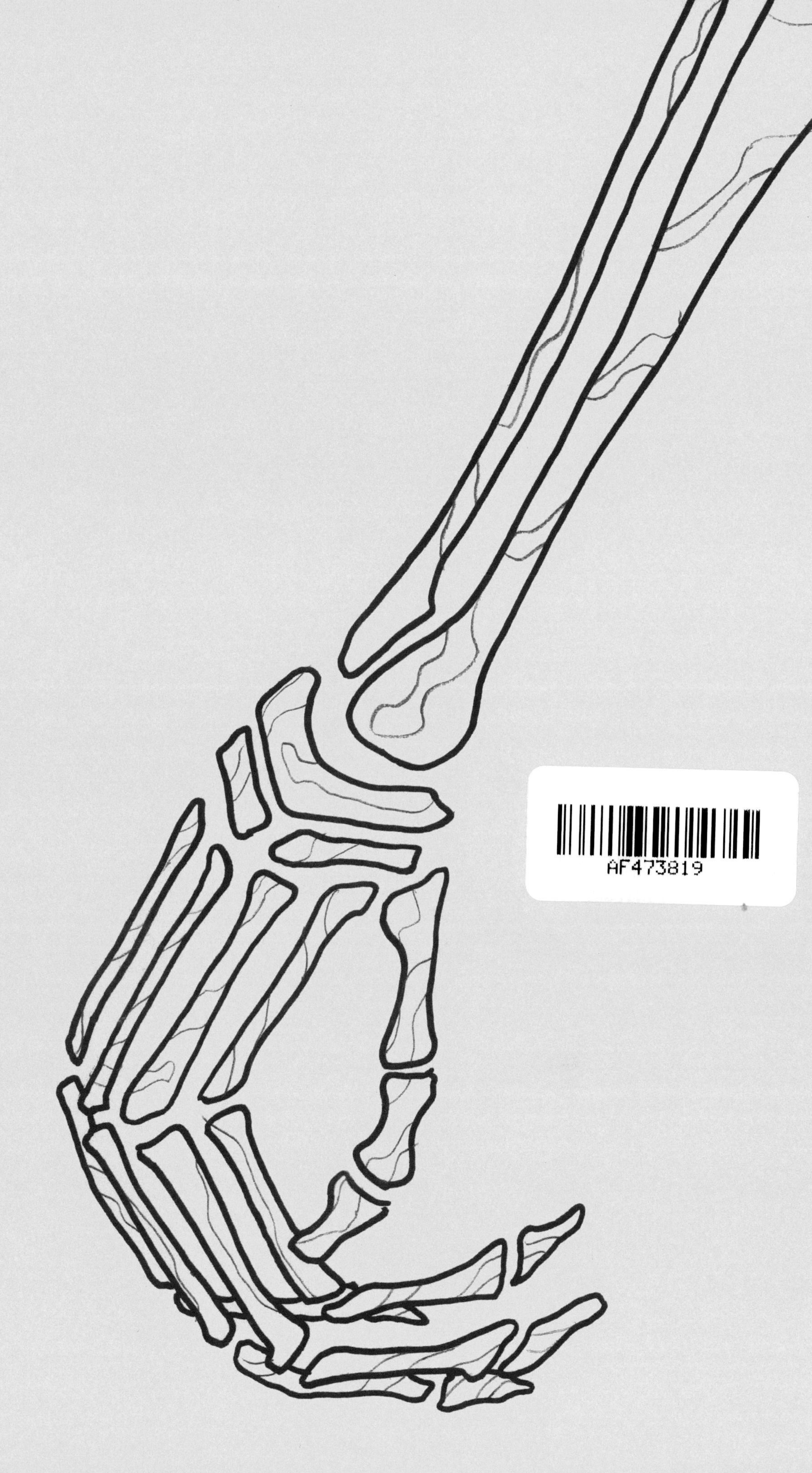

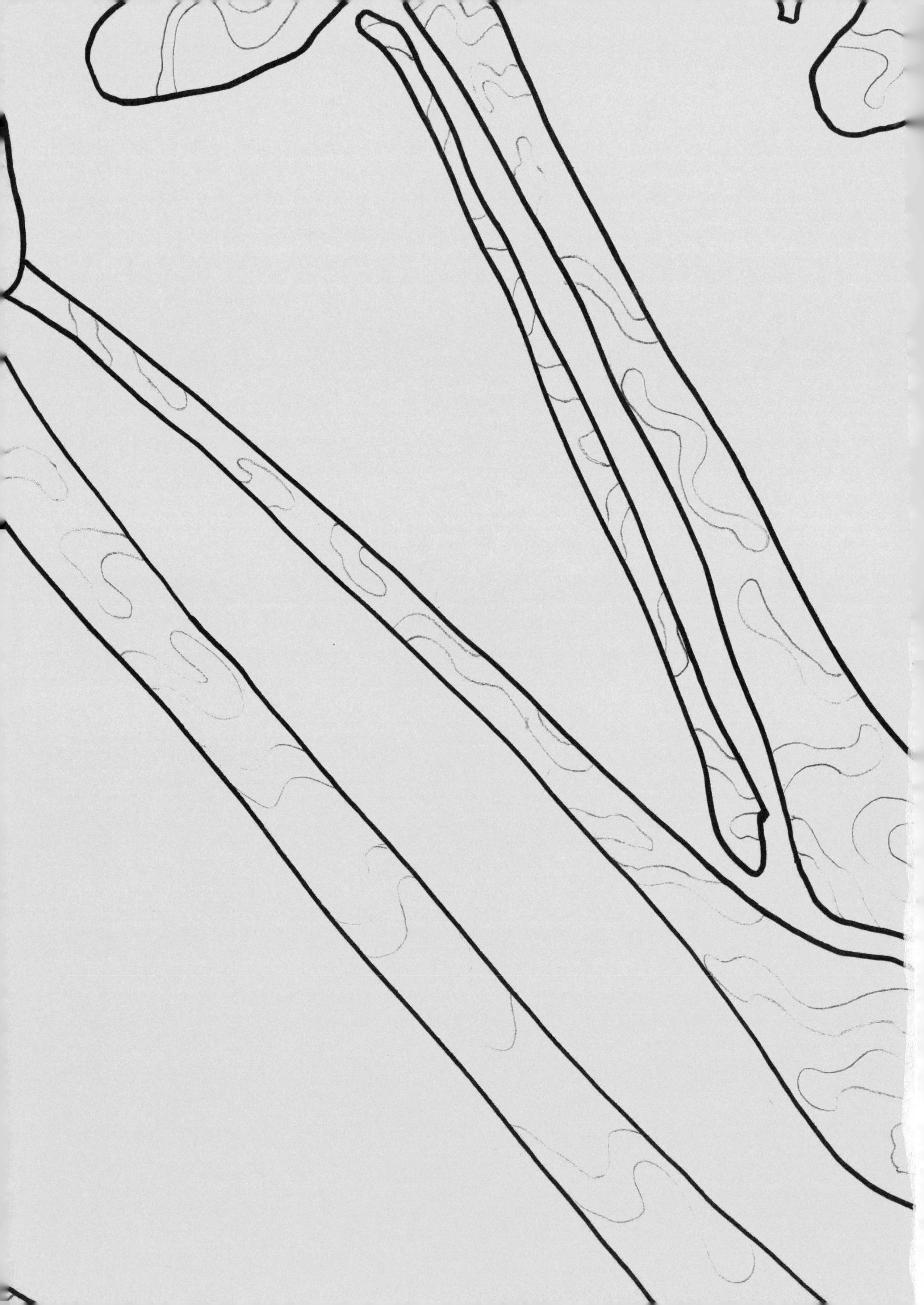

Gina Proenza

Musée cantonal des Beaux-Arts
Lausanne

jrp|editions

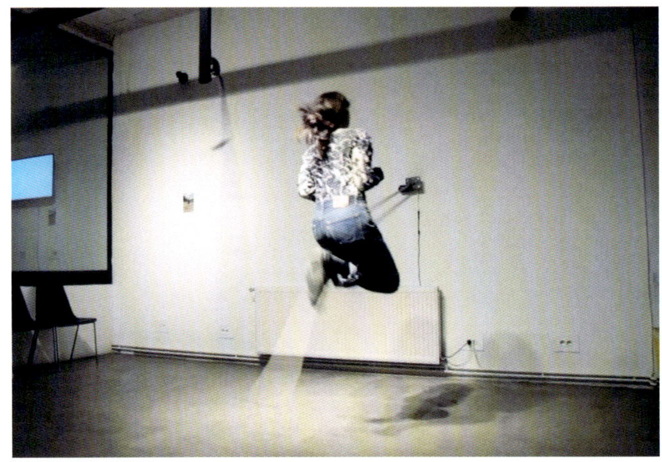

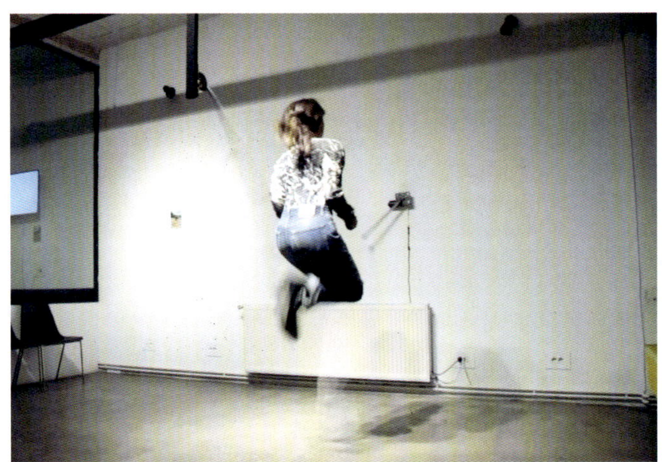

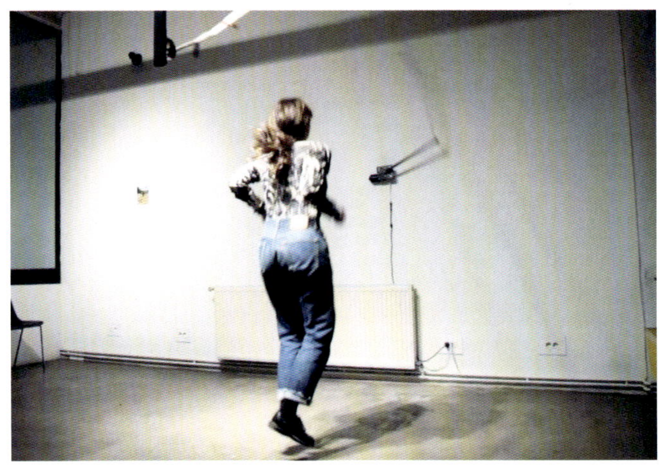

Fealing Station, 2019

Gina Proenza: Balancing Act

Nicole Schweizer

> "This love—almost desperate, but charged with tenderness—that you must show for your tightrope, will have as much strength as the metal wire that carries you. I know objects, their malignancy, their cruelty, their gratitude, too. The wire was dead—or if you like, mute, blind—but now that you are here, it will live and speak [...] Who, before you, ever realized how much nostalgia resides in the core of a seven-millimeter steel wire?"[1]

A gargoyle of plaster and lacquered wood, sticking out a slowly wagging tongue; a motorized jump rope tracing large circles; a wooden floor that destabilizes anybody who walks across it; benches in wood or metal that swing up and down; jaguar heads sporting frilly collars and knotted satin fabrics that stream from their open jaws, ending in a spoon that twirls at various speeds; and a mesh curtain that glides through space ...

Gina Proenza's works move. Or, if they remain motionless, her works make the body move within the installation space. A reflection in a mirror, or words arranged on an abacus, or a skeleton of embroidered straw dancing on three legs, or spinning-tops concealing hidden faces: everything urges us to move forward, backward, or around, or else to halt, thereby creating a slow and subtle ballet of bodies whose choreography is as important as the dance of the gaze. This haptic relationship to objects is accentuated by the artist's careful attention to materials employed, whether they are constructed, found, appropriated, or subverted. They are sometimes soft and warm like polished wood, sometimes cold and slick like glazed porcelain, at other times rough, translucent, or luminous. There is little or no sound, yet everything hums. Not only because motors make tongues wag, spoons gently twirl, and curtains move, nor because our footfalls resonate on the sprung floor, nor because we make the swinging benches squeak when we sit on them. More importantly, if less tangibly, all these materials hum with stories. Stories occupying the fold between the formal tradition of minimalist sculptures and the narratives inhabiting them, or arising from the weave of memories, fictions, found texts, historic documents, Caribbean legends, and European tales that inspired them.

1
Jean Genet, "The Tightrope Walker," in *Fragments of the Artwork,* trans. Charlotte Mandell, Stanford University Press, Stanford 2003, p. 69–70; translation slightly modified here.

Sometimes words surge forth as simple sounds or onomatopoeia; at other times they compose phrases inscribed on an abacus, a light box, a weave of straw, or a stroboscopic projection whose hectic pace blurs interpretation and sharpens the heartbeat. And a narrative takes place—a narrative found not just in the objects themselves, but also in the gap between them, in the space they inhabit for the duration of an exhibition. The artist herself identifies with in-betweenness—between one word and another, between a work and its installation, between Colombia (where she was born) and France (where she later grew up), between two continents with their respective traditions and interwoven histories. Whose threads have to be unraveled again in order to find one's way.

"Why do we need to tell—or tell ourselves—stories, and how do we do that?"[2] If Proenza has chosen an essentially visual language in order to communicate, articulating the phrasing of each of her shows through a specific grammar of objects, it is probably due to the polysemic potential of that language. Every object has its own story, but at the same time it becomes a protagonist in the particular narrative of each installation. Proenza thus refers to her exhibitions as different articulations of similar stories.[3]

In her current project for the Musée cantonal des Beaux-Arts de Lausanne, Proenza gives voice to different versions of a single story. The story in question is a true one of cases brought by ecclesiastic courts in the Lausanne region in the 15th and 16th centuries against the insects that destroyed harvests. Entitled *Toi et ta bande* (You and Your Gang, 2024), this work, composed of several voices, interrogates the stances of those people who either issue or receive a sentence; it displaces the speaking subject in order to give the floor to those denied it; it creates space for rethinking what can occur between apparently distant periods, between theoretically distant species. Like a knot whose potential strands are unraveled, here Proenza's primary material is a historical source that has already inspired other recent research.[4] While the form adopted in the installation space still wavers between multiple possibilities, the new shift occurs in the rewriting of the narrative itself, in a reinterpretation that resonates with our times. "Nowadays, these accounts may seem completely irrational or fictional to us. At the same time, they echo highly contemporary problematics: inter-species cohabitation, the ecological emergency, and lawsuits that tend to grant legal standing to entities like rivers, for example."[5] Attentive to the texture of every element, to the weight of bodies as well as of words, to the light or serious tone of their combination, and to the way they resonate with "the time that remains,"[6] Gina Proenza is moving forward, balancing herself through our present times.

2
Gina Proenza, *Vertigo*, radio broadcast, Radio Télévision Suisse, August 16, 2023.

3
Interview with the artist, November 2, 2023.

4
Catherine Chêne, "Juger les vers: exorcismes et procès d'animaux dans le diocèse de Lausanne (XVe-XVIe siècles)," *Cahiers lausannois d'histoire médiévale* 14 (1995), Université de Lausanne.

5
Gina Proenza in Rinny Gremaud, "Gina Proenza, plasticienne à l'âme de scénographe, qui sculpte avec des mots," *Le Temps*, Lausanne, February 26, 2023, https://www.letemps.ch/culture/gina-proenza-plasticienne-lame-scenographe-sculpte-mots (last accessed April 2024).

6
Patrick Boucheron, *Le Temps qui reste*, Le Seuil, Paris 2023.

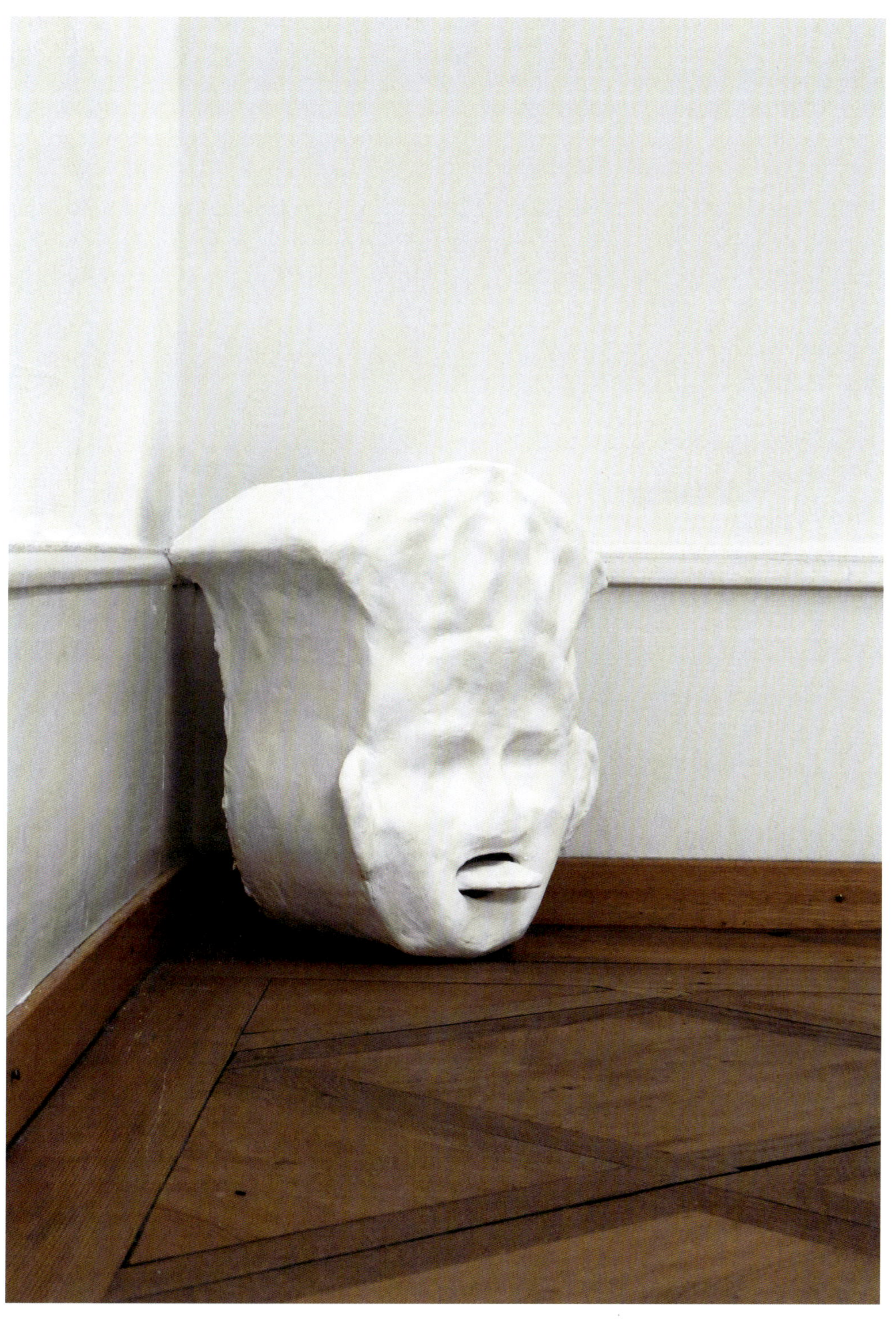

Le Rut animal, 2017

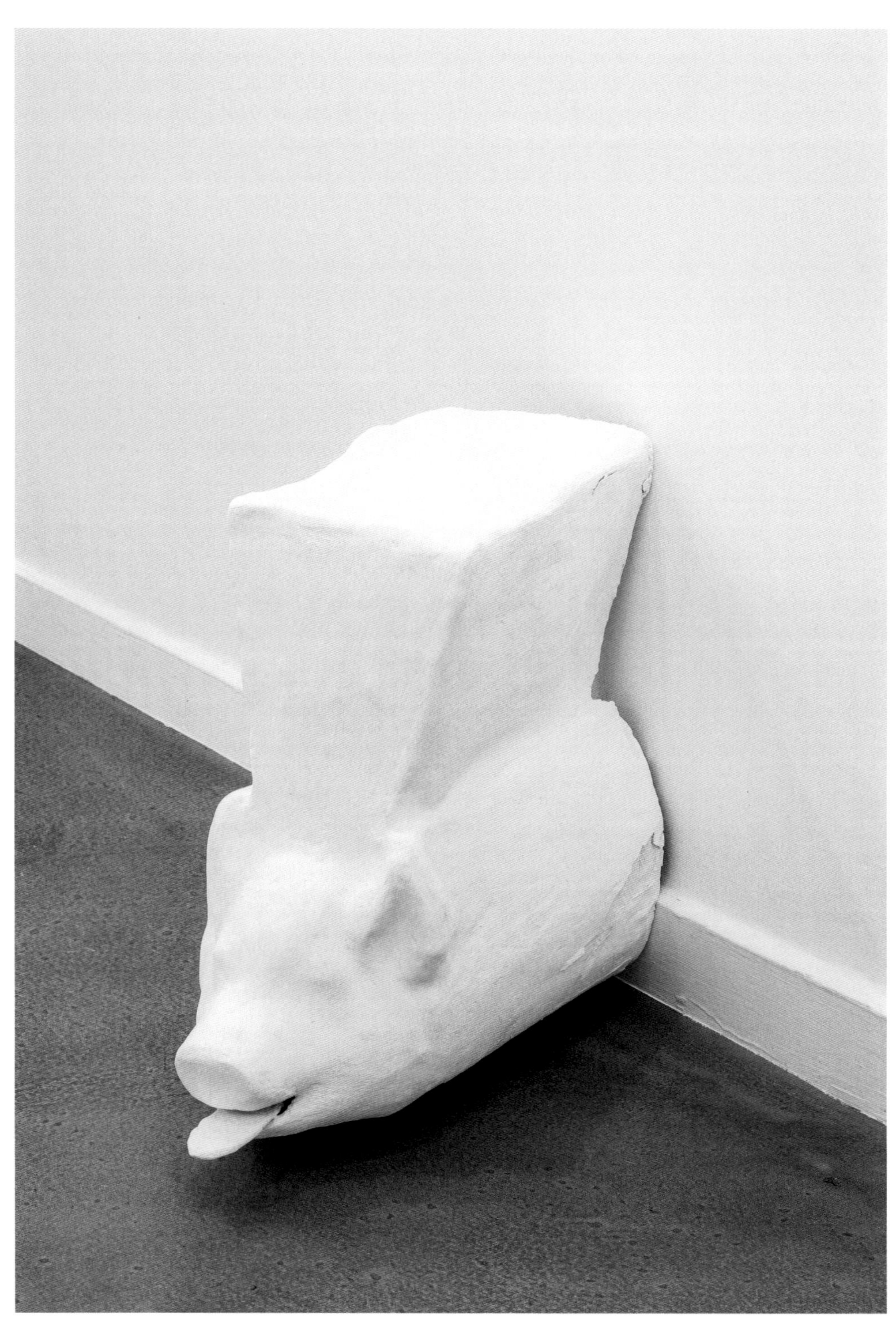

L'Ami naturel, 2017

Protesting and Erotic Tongues: Gina Proenza's Concrete Dialectic

Salome Hohl

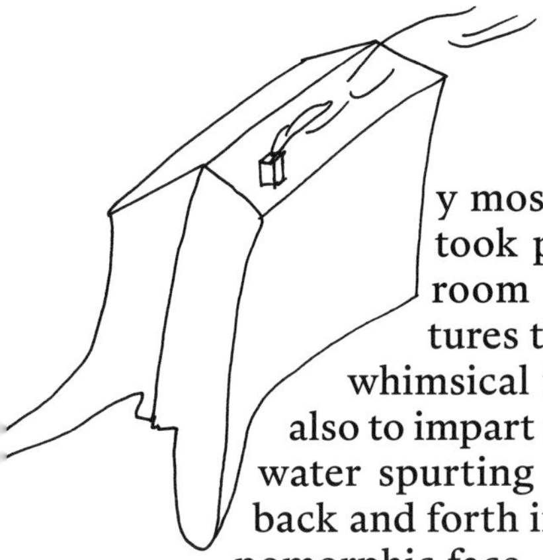

My most significant encounter with Gina Proenza's art took place at the Kunsthaus Langenthal. In the first room of her three-part exhibition were two sculptures that reminded me of medieval gargoyles—those whimsical figures that serve not only to divert water, but also to impart moral messages and ward off evil. But instead of water spurting from their maws, mechanical tongues moved back and forth in the openings of the pig's head and the anthropomorphic face. At first it seemed as if they were sticking their tongues out at me. On closer inspection, however, they appeared more to interact silently with one another, and it remained unclear whether they were amusing themselves, flirting, or repelling each other.

That was in February 2018, in the context of the nomadic exhibition series *Plattform18*. I have, since then, strongly associated tongue sculptures with Proenza, not simply because they recur in her exhibitions. They put the spotlight on fundamental forms of speech and silence, dialogue, physical intimacy, and gestural refusal, all of which are core themes in the artist's practice. The message of these figures also revealed an ambiguity: did they seek to exclude or include me? Was their communication based on a dynamic of welcome or rejection? What historical and cultural context did I attribute to them?

The title of this 2017 work, *L'Ami naturel* (Natural Friend), is an heteropalindrome that conceals the words "Le rut animal" (animal rutting) when read backward, reinforcing this interpretation. It made me wonder—to what extent do attraction or humor function as vehicles of communication, and how are reading perspectives, specific moments of interpretation, and sites of speaking linked. Speaking is closely linked to actions, which do not take a linear course, but develop, emerge, and disappear in communities and spaces. Statements always reflect attitudes or emotional states. These thoughts are certainly suggested by the motif of the tongue, which symbolizes ambiguity, embodying both wisdom and truth as well as mockery and protest. The tongue is seen as a carrier of disease and a sensual site of eroticism, and is the preferred organ for figures stylized as monsters or fools.

In Proenza's complex installations, sculptures such as *L'Ami naturel* are woven into a network of different narratives that are realized in various media. At *Plattform18* in Langenthal, the artist conceived the artworks following her research in Palenque de San Basilio, a Colombian village founded in the 17th century by escaped slaves who built an autonomous community in a remote area and developed the Palenquero language—a mixture of Portuguese, Spanish, and African Bantu languages. This endows *L'Ami naturel* with an additional dimension: "speaking all tongues" is an ability to speak several languages, while "speaking in tongues" stands for unintelligible speech. Besides the metaphorical meaning of speaking obscurely and not being understood, there is also a literal meaning here, namely communicating in several languages. Palenquero is subversive, a true jumble of languages that radiates an identity-building power inwardly, and outwardly functions as a defense against colonial rule. This perspective raises general questions, such as: when and how does listening and understanding happen? What significance do different languages have, and to what extent does language promote community? In a sense, this perspective reinforces the position of these sculptures as gatekeepers of their own world, as symbols of resistance, and as a protective barrier.

This dimension was also evident in the next room: the monumental sculptures, bathed in yellow and covered in a glaze that smelled of wood, could be described as trees, wooden fortresses, or—because of their narrow opening—surreal letterboxes [p. 50–51]. Even without the knowledge of the story of this Colombian village, the wooden modules felt like something that shield or protect. They structured encounters and invited the adoption of different positions of reception. These characteristics can be found in numerous works by Proenza, starting with her 2017 diploma project at ECAL (Lausanne), which consisted of a wall installation in that poisonous shade of green that can be erased or replaced in film post-production, with window-like cutouts that enabled an interplay between screening and transparency. They were also reminiscent of lopsided dwellings or barricades during riots. But what does it mean when, as here, the background can be edited at will? Three small gray monkeys sat on the modules, bringing to mind the proverb "see no evil, hear no evil, speak no evil." Loudspeakers, which emitted a kind of lullaby, replaced their heads. The lyrics of the lullaby were based on an interview with a physicist talking about the concept of emptiness. The work conveyed a feeling of disorientation and meaningless communication strategies.

This interplay between dissimulation and revelation, between observing and being observed, is again at work in the transparent gray curtain that moved mechanically throughout Proenza's solo exhibition at the Kunst Halle Sankt Gallen in 2023 [p. 26–29]. With this veil-like textile she extended her gesture to a charged (also erotically) theatrical and art-historical tradition: the textile conceals what is to be presented, but as a visual obstacle it highlights what is hidden. The barrier allowed Proenza to influence the audience's possible walking and viewing paths, which changed continuously as a result of the mechanical movement. This begs the question of who belongs on the stage or in the exhibition, and who takes on what role. Are the visitors or the works of art in the spotlight? In general, Proenza's approach to her work demonstrates that the artist incorporates interaction into her conception: how can the attendees help shape the narrative? How do they react to dividing lines? How stable are the visual axes and paths? Some works show this directly, such as the moving floors of *Social Gravity*, also presented at the Kunst Halle Sankt Gallen, on which visitors could rest, engage in motion, or balance.

In a figurative sense, this balancing act can also lead one to question the grounds of knowledge or belief on which one is standing. Who cuts a good figure on which floor? When the ground shakes underfoot, who takes responsibility? Which communities shape our understanding of having our "feet on the ground"? This, at least, is how I connected the moving floors with the narrative that ran through the Kunst Halle Sankt Gallen, where Proenza made use of a historical example to examine the context-dependent use of language and its performative power. Relying on surviving documents from archives in the cantons of Fribourg and Vaud, she thematized a historical case in which, during a famine in the 15th and 16th centuries, the larvae of the chafer beetle were blamed for a crop failure, and the "pests" were then legally banned from the fields. The artist gathered available archival texts on this criminal trial, and rearranged words such as "annihilation," "appropriate," and "excommunication" alphabetically to reveal the repetition of frequently used words and shared values that are tied to language. She took words used in the trial, such as "Toi et ta bande" (You and your gang), or "the infamous" and "the beasts," and wrote them in letters made of straw. Transposing this to the contemporary context prompts thoughts such as: if we can no longer point to bugs, who will we blame for climate change? What actions result from this, and what language do we use for them? Here it is evident that language possesses a reality-altering power.

The experimentation with signs, phonemes, and shifts in meaning also manifests itself in Proenza's light box works, which are often part of her exhibitions. The letters o a o a could be read on one such panel on view in Langenthal and at ECAL. Originally a Coca-Cola light box, this found object can be interpreted as a symbol of globalization, in which market and power structures are linked. The name "Coca" refers to a plant from South America that is of great importance to indigenous communities, while "Cola" is an African nut. Both terms in the name of the American company refer to colonial gestures. By removing the consonants from the light box, Proenza deprives the brand of its advertising impact and reduces it to the core of the Latin language: the vowels. Proenza's games with communication processes seem never to let up; they are always in motion, yet firmly anchored as tangible art objects. The tongue as a metaphor for language functions as a mediator between all the things that stand in relation to one another. They open up channels of communication in which the repertoire of verbal and non-verbal means of expression is revealed. Proenza's works of art constantly shift stories and perspectives into new constellations. This also raises the question: if we are able to change narratives and establish different forms of contact, can we also shape reality? This idea sheds light on the power of stories, viewing them not only as mirrors that reflect reality, but also as tools for shaping and transforming it.

Perhaps this is why there are also references to the Middle Ages and the early modern period in her work. In this era, explanations often took the form of allegorical narratives. Those who told stories in such a way that they could be vividly experienced had power. This thirst—in life, in works of art, and in the theater—for cathartic moments, symbolic interpretations, and guardian figures and fools, as well as eschatological ideas, has not been exhausted to this day. The longing persists for an extensive vocabulary for playing with interpretations, exploring hidden dialogues, and developing new perspectives. In her art, Proenza provides a broad, tangible vocabulary with which visitors can sensitize and expand their perception of the world, of speaking, and of listening. In this context I am reminded again of the phenomenon of "speaking in tongues," where someone having a spiritual experience speaks a language that is not directly comprehensible to themselves or to others present. Perhaps Proenza's works of art are such "speaking (in) tongues" in a double sense: firstly, "speaking in tongues" as an act that transcends our experiential horizon of the crisis-ridden present, opens up new perspectives, and speaks in a prophetic and visionary way; and secondly, "speaking tongues" as an opening up of multilingual political dialogue, somewhere between eroticism and protest, named social injustices, and humorous *Terrain Vague*.

Traductrice cleptomane, 2020 →

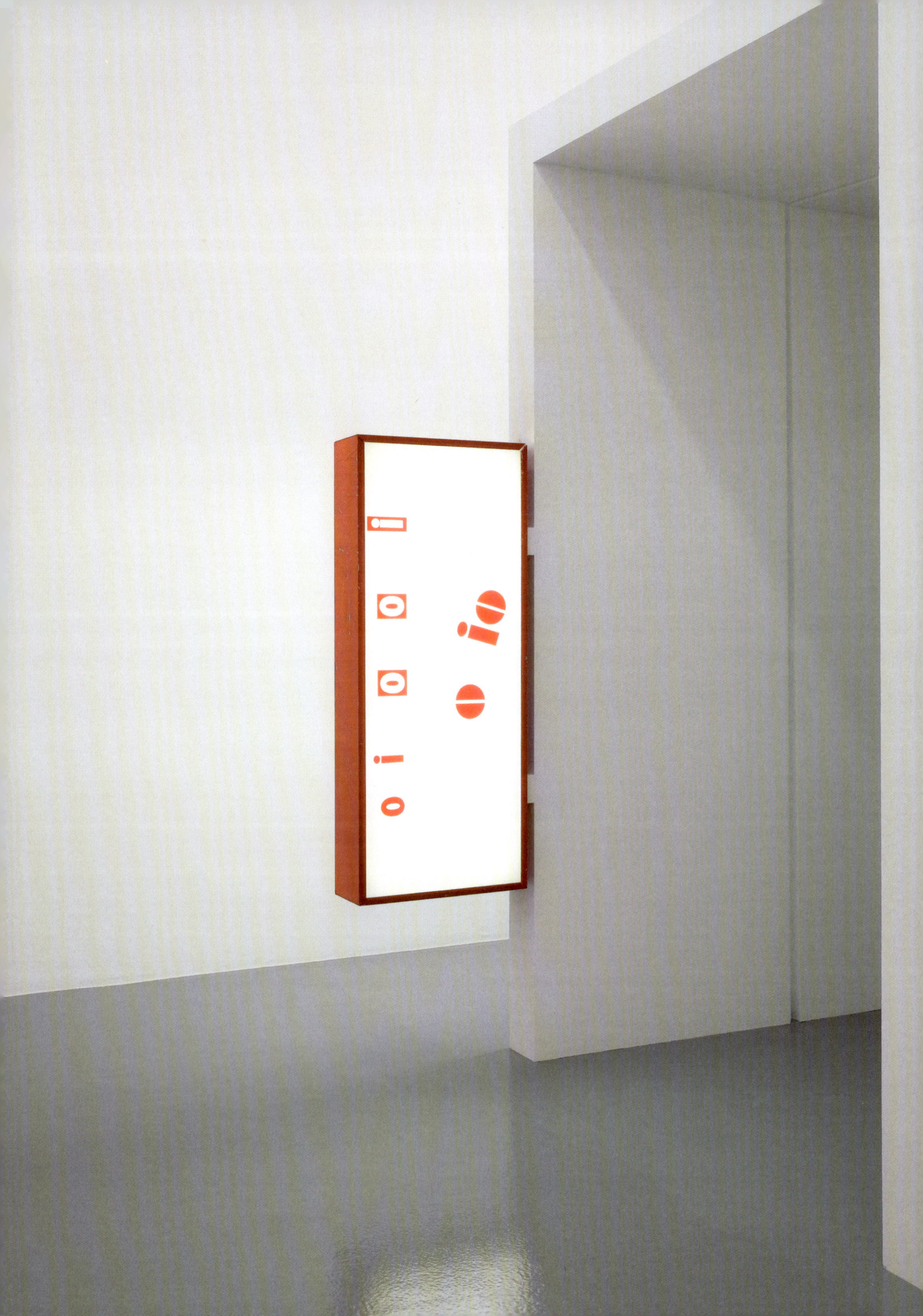

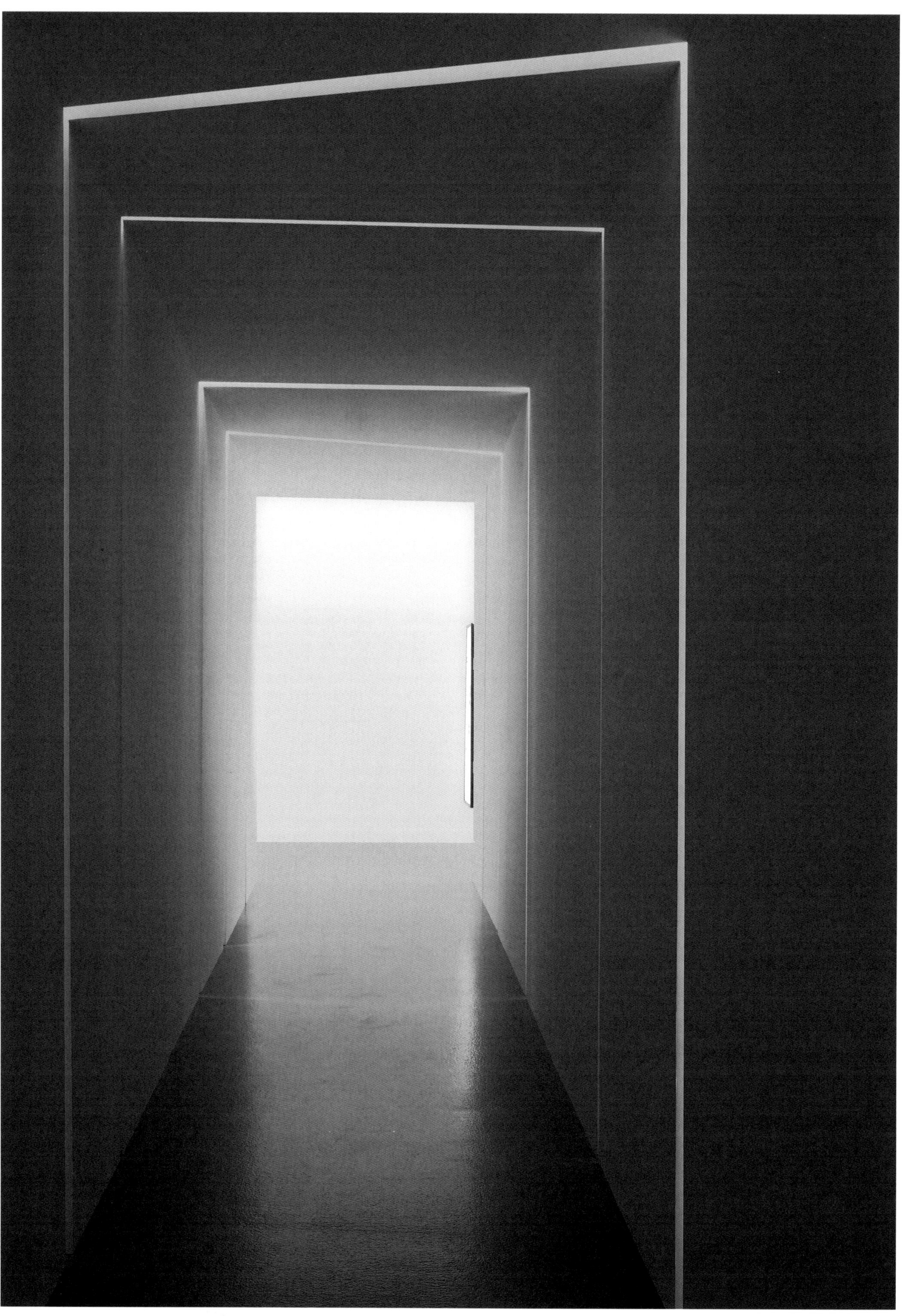

Agarra-diablo, 2020

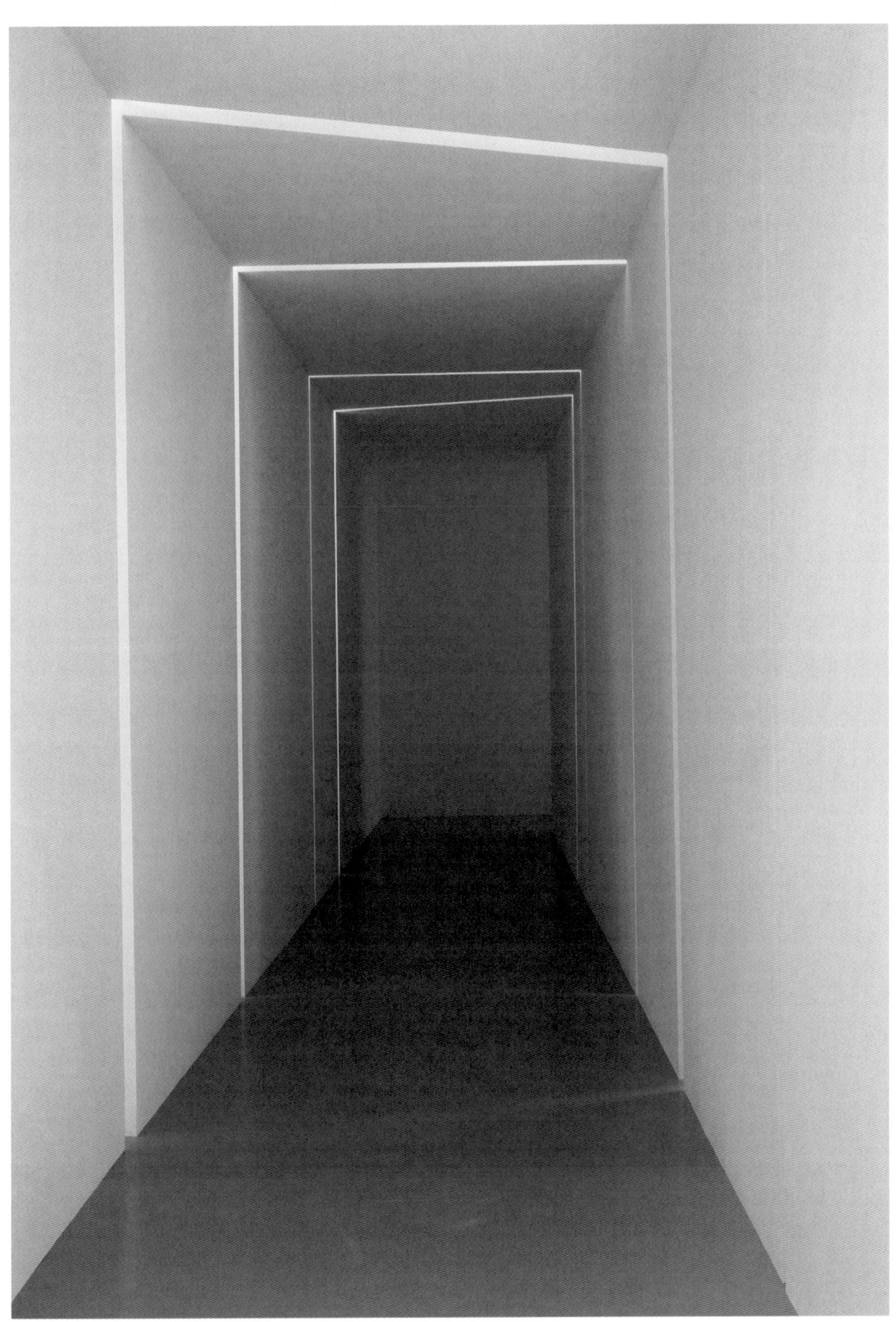

Agarra-diablo, 2020

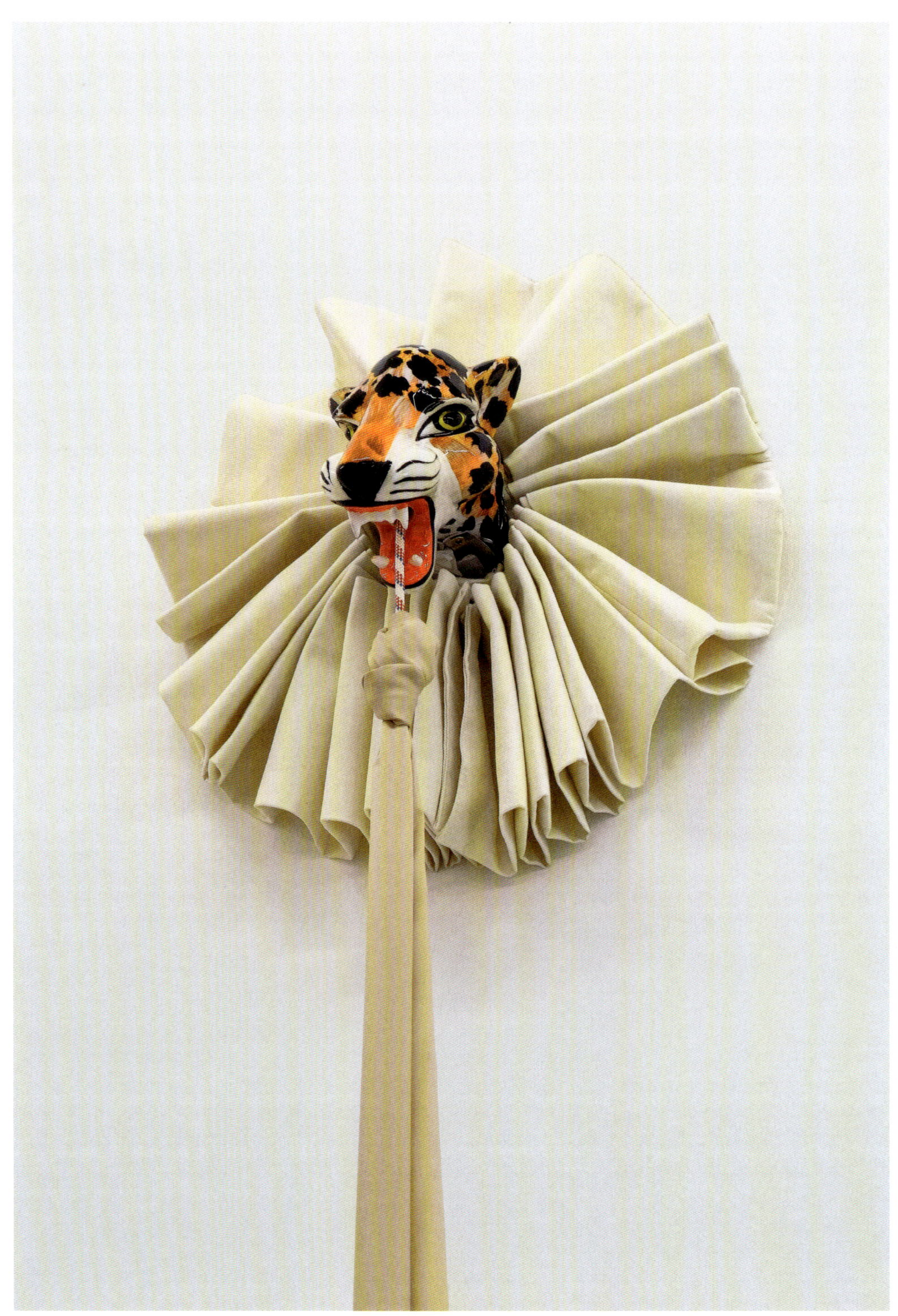

L'Ami naturel I, 2020
Nostalgie en pantoufles (Social Gravity), 2020 →

Nr.1062

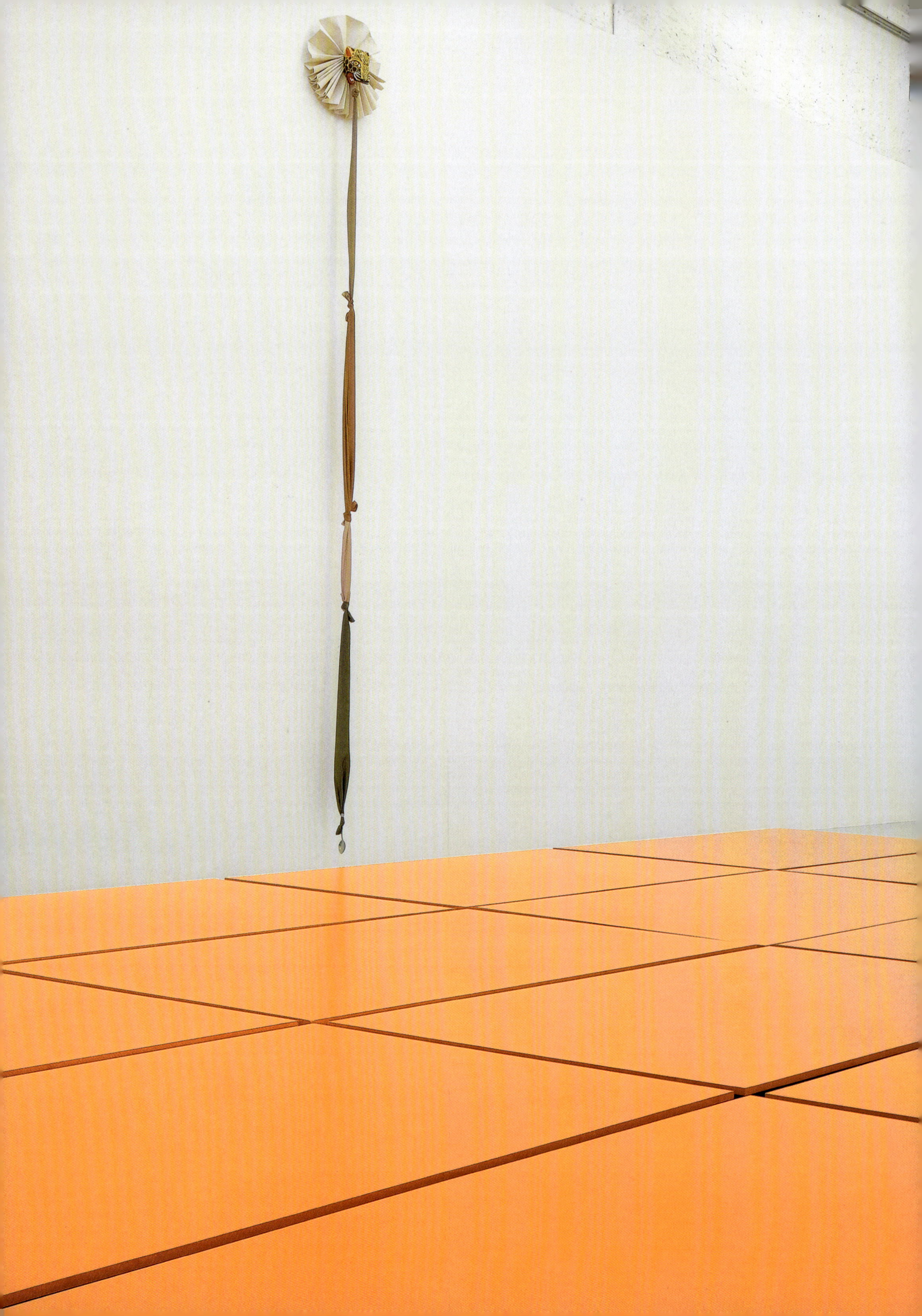

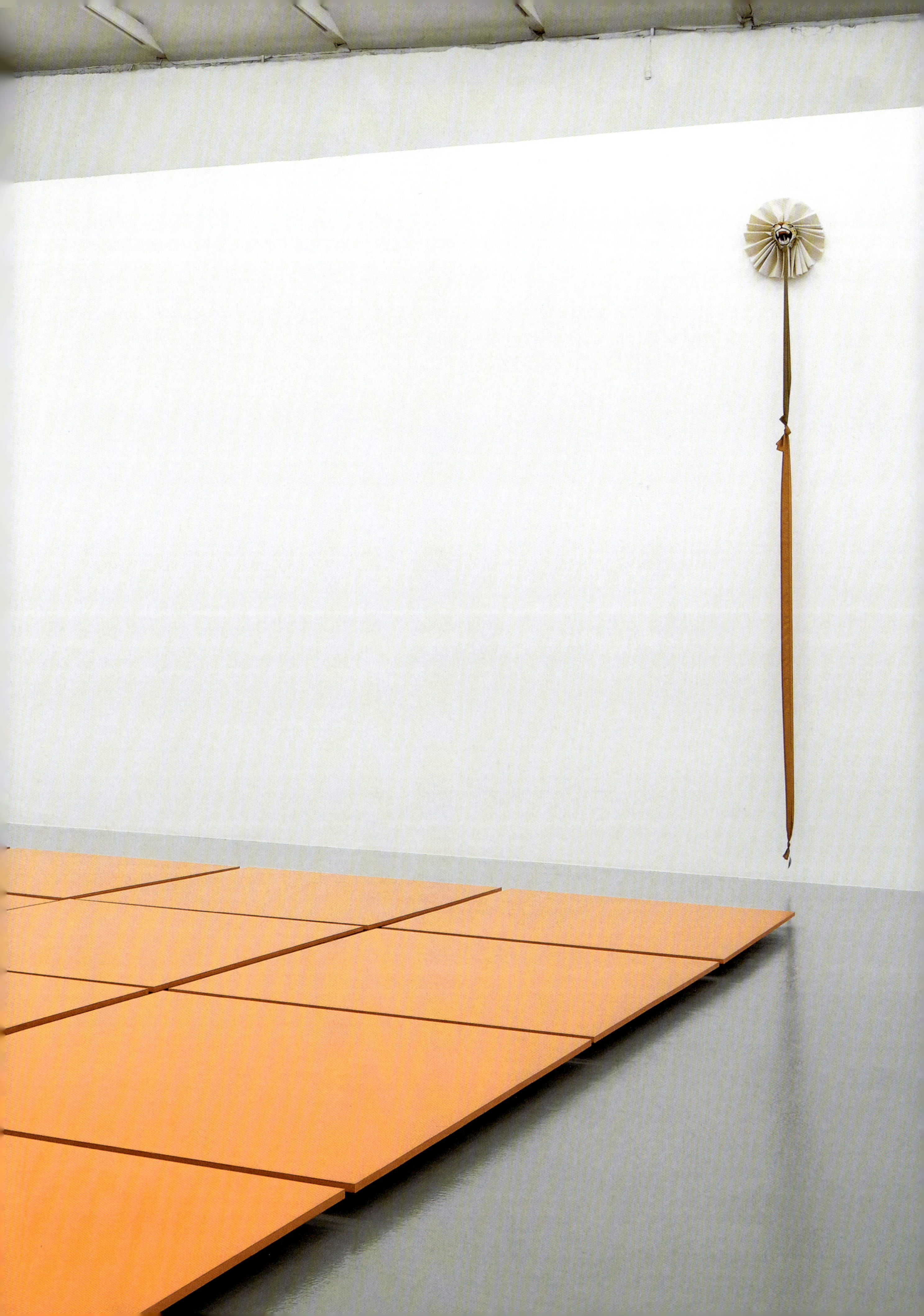

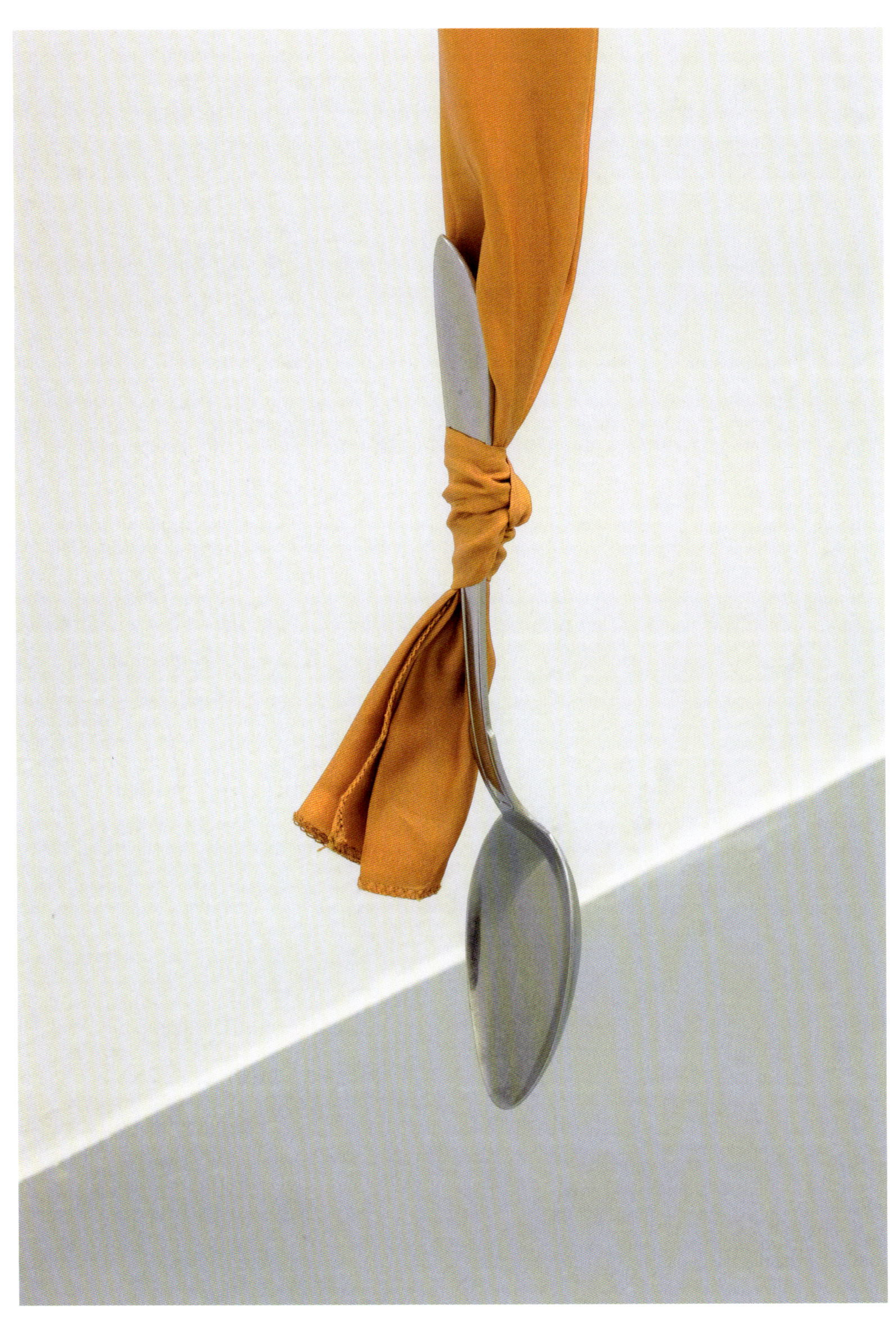

L'Ami naturel II, 2020
← *Agarra-diablo*, CAN, Neuchâtel, 2020

Lacking Words, Misspelling Others

Gina Proenza In Conversation with Nicolas Brulhart

SWAYING GROUND?

NB Your exhibitions often begin with powerful installations that enable you to appropriate the space. In *Passe Passe* (Centre culturel suisse, Paris, 2018) and *Agarra-diablo* (CAN–Centre d'art Neuchâtel, 2020) you "carpeted" the area with a swaying ground created by brightly colored wooden structures. You also like to employ other structures that flirt with exhibition design: passageways, sliding curtains, handrails, trap doors, and swinging benches.

GP By constructing floors that sway, I imply that the same piece of ground has to be shared, that everyone is subjected to a common balance and gravity. When I exhibited them for the first time in Paris, I was struck by the dialogues they created among people, ranging from an exchange of glances to verbal conversation, indeed to collective decisions ("suppose everybody moves to the left" or "to each corner"). Inviting people to walk inside a corridor or on unstable ground, or making a wall piece pivot, is a way for me to make contact—which corresponds to an idealized, artificial wish to play with tactile forms, inviting people to touch the works, themselves, or others. It's an attempt to affect their bodies, to rethink their interactions and interdependency, by creating zones for pausing, conversing, or resting.

NB You seem to be playing on the appeal of comfort, accessibility, and hiding places in a dialectic that makes approaching an artwork a more tangible experience.

GP In almost all my shows there are slits, openings, or false bottoms, as though things hesitate to reveal their form completely. By making people want to see the other side—or inside—I exploit the hidden face of things, sparking a desire to know more. It's a straightforward way of stimulating the imagination, yet also of resisting any immediate understanding, any static, overall grasp of things.

NB This approach connects with a heritage of kinetic, minimal, and neo-concrete art, with the history of interactivity. In the 1960s, those art forms emerged on several different continents, and therefore their social horizon differed, from Europe to the United States and South America. I'm thinking of the mazes created by GRAV (Groupe de Recherche d'Art Visuel), of Hélio Oiticica's *Penetrables*, of the environments created by Jesús Rafael Soto and Carlos Cruz-Diez, and of Lygia Clark's *bichos*.

GP Clark's *bichos* are sculptures that can be handled and constantly transformed—their forms are never fixed. I always felt they were thumbing their noses at certain minimalist sculptures made in the United States at that time. That period also represented the years of the revolutionary Left in Abya Yala or so-called Latin America, from the Cuban revolution (1953–1959) to the early guerrilla movements in Colombia (FARC, ELN, and others in the 1960s), to the presidential election of Salvador Allende in Chile (1970). Those political narratives populated my childhood, and I was heavily marked by the resulting cultural expressions of insurrection, resistance, and escape.

NB Those art movements probably didn't carry the same meaning, depending on the context in which they arose. I get the impression that you're interested in their intersections and the resulting confusions.

GP You referred to artists whose work seems fueled by the dynamics of digestion, along the lines of the *Anthropophagic Manifesto* (1928) by Brazilian poet Oswald de Andrade, who in the early 20th century proposed feeding off colonial cultures the better to free himself from them. More recently, in her first film (*Reassemblage,* 1982), the filmmaker Trinh T. Minh Ha said, "I do not intend to speak about; just to speak nearby." By insisting on this distance, she decided to leave a gap, some room, so that others could position themselves even as she situated her own gaze. I find that stance fascinating, and I try to adopt the same method, attempting to look or listen *near* the materials or people I work with.

NB Take one of your works such as the rain stick (*Agarra-diablo*, 2020): it's an object inscribed within a culture, imbued with a power that hinges on certain beliefs. Once exhibited, it inevitably becomes part of a formalist or abstract discourse. In your work there's the idea of playing on the function of an object, which triggers a dilemma of interpretation, or rather allows the coexistence of interpretations that aesthetic tradition would view as opposing.

GP *Agarra-diablo* was composed of a long corridor with artificial perspectives and a hanging object that swiveled when clothing or bodies brushed against it, creating the sound of a storm, like a warning, or a trap. In the exhibition, the sound of rain indicated a human presence. The entire show was about the coexistence of double functions: sculpture-rituals were simultaneously games and artworks, methods of surveillance and eavesdropping that were non-functional. The title *Agarra-diablo* comes in fact from the name of a plant with abrasive, tearing qualities, which can be used as a natural wall or forest stronghold that both protects and imprisons.

NB *Rassemblées (Suto)* (2018) and *Jalousies modernes* (2021) are installations of painted geometrical wooden structures with slits at eye-level.

GP Maybe those holes create the impression of being watched. As though perhaps the rules of encounter are being reversed.

NB There's nothing neutral about such exchanges. On the contrary, they stress the asymmetry of the relationship—they challenge the autonomy of the modern eye, which takes things in but gives nothing in return.

GP In the *Rassemblées (Suto)* installation (Kunsthaus Langenthal, 2018), the positioning of works played hide-and-seek with eye and body. The spatial arrangement alluded to strategies of resistance and hiding by slaves from the Colombian Caribbean on the run in the 17th and 18th centuries, while also assuming some of the proportions of the furnishings of Western parliaments, where imperialist governments exercised power.

NB Your mechanized tongues and eyes (*L'Ami naturel,* 2017–2023) create a feeling that I think is central to your work: strangeness. These pieces are provocative and attractive, but they also render suspect the amused gaze that neutralizes them.

GP The tongues move in and out of mouths of plaster, wood, or porcelain, or from inside a wall. These works parody the irreverent act of sticking your tongue out. They are sculptures that mock their own role and their surroundings.

NB The mechanism makes them seem disdainful. Their movement violates a taboo, disrupting the solemnity of sculpture that alludes to vestiges of civilizations in a temporal transposition. They also create an aura of the fantastic.

GP People often mention the sensual side of these licking tongues, which I find very funny because nothing seems less erotic to me than a movement produced by a windshield-wiper motor—regular and repetitive.

NB Yet we're familiar with the eroticism of technology via the concept of fetishism. By making movement and life-likeness mechanical, you interrogate the complicated relationship between fetishism (of merchandise) and animism.

GP There's a passage I love in Ursula K. Le Guin's novel, *The Dispossessed* (1974), where a character experiences the capitalist world and the erotic quality of the objects comprising it for the first time. The smooth textures of seats and the curves of handrails on staircases seem designed to spark desire and arousal. I look for those relationships between humans and technology by using motors to move imitation parts of the body and by making a skipping rope twirl between two walls rather than between hands.

WHICH TONGUES ARE SPEAKING WHICH LANGUAGES?

NB How would you describe the role of language in your work?

GP It represents a desire to multiply languages, to seek the borderlines of language, in tropes such as onomatopoeia and puns. This plurality also exists in the dialogues I instigate when I work, for example, by producing the scent of emptiness with a professional nose, or by filming a "zoo curator" talking about the management of their "collection," or by ordering chemically modified paint, or by asking a marching band to parade through the galleries of a museum ... For that matter, I extend this approach into my teaching, exhibition organizing, and commitment to independent art scenes.

NB In addition to this collective dimension, the tongues—among other metonyms of language in your work—create a tension around the act of speaking or not speaking, as though these works are stressing their inability to recount a tale.

GP For me, the act of story-telling perhaps resides in the strange anagram between conserve and converse, conservation and conversation. There's perpetual motion, oscillating between the need to recount in order to remember, and the desire to keep the dialogue open in order to thwart the fear of pinning down or petrifying any one version of the story.

NB The transparent language of communication began crumbling very early on in your work, with the light boxes—*o a o a* (2017), *Nu/Un* (2020), *Patron/Partner* (2022), *No/Ou* (2023), *Dead/Dad DNA* (2023)—where consonants often get lost, and only lilting vowels remain, which don't allow the language to form words.

GP Those light boxes are found objects that I clean up and repair, removing a few letters in order to blur the advertising message written there. The brand messages are thereby transformed into onomatopoeia, or shouts, or the vocal exercises of opera castrati, or the babbling of babies.

NB Some of your recent works merge language with the visual dimension of art: abacus-texts, wisps of straw-words, verbal projections, and so on.

GP Yes, the letters emerge from the materials themselves, some are made of straw, or wooden beads, or light. Sometimes the source text itself becomes the material, the clay to be molded. Lately, for example, I've been sorting certain journalistic or documentary articles into alphabetical order. When filing them, I list the number of times words appear and are repeated.

NB One title, *Traductrice cleptomane* (2020), seems to push this wordplay to an extreme. The relationship between words and things extends to inversions, substitutions, and mutual confiscation.

GP That title echoes a short story by the Hungarian writer Dezsö Kosztaolányi, *The Kleptomaniac Translator* (1933), which tells the tale of a poet who finds himself stealing items of value within fiction. When translating crime novels from English into his native tongue, he steals watches, jewelry, cars. Theft is also a mode of production, a stealing of ideas and forms by using or valorizing; for example, the influence an entourage or environment can have on the production of a work.

NB Your more recent work with straw uses that material, with its power and natural presence, to form a slogan, *Toi et ta bande* (You and Your Gang, 2023). For me, this work ironically alludes to the tendency of contemporary art to function in a herd way.

GP *Toi et ta bande* are words that emerge from the abundant straw, playing on the parody of a trompe-l'oeil or landscape painting. "You and your gang" is a modern rendition of a legal decree issued when medieval lawsuits were brought against a type of worm. The invertebrates were accused of destroying harvests and causing great famine. The sentence was read out loud in fields of grain around Lausanne, and began with these words: "Thou and thy company have created considerable damage to the soil: you have six days to vacate the premises." *Toi et ta bande* is an ambiguous form of address, oscillating between the individual and the group. Can all members of the same group identify with this "thou-you/me," or does it imply a vertical hierarchy with a single leader?

NB That's a way of raising a key problematic in today's art, I think, namely: knowing who is speaking in whose name and to whom. Your installations often involve issues of various lands and who occupies them, with their layered histories and the issues of power that result.

GP I feel a special attachment to lands or territories whose occupation has been unstable, such as the region of Darién, on the border between Colombia and Panama, which notably inspired the exhibition *Agarra-diablo*. I'm fascinated by that area because it seems to have resisted all forms of colonization. Ever since the 15th century, imperialist powers have tried and failed to completely subjugate the native populations and lands. It's a place that certain governments consider off-limits, and yet it's illegally crossed every day, now being one of the most important routes for migrants.

NB Does the fact that we can go back to your sources have any importance, or don't they have any value in themselves?

GP They serve above all as starting points, a little like summoning up spirits and then expecting all kinds of incarnations to emerge; they're skeletons whose coverings still have to be concocted. The narratives behind—or before—the works sometimes become a distant murmur, like ghosts who haunt the exhibitions and titles of artworks.

FRIENDS IN COMMON

NB I wanted to bring up certain titles, such as *L'Ami naturel* (Natural Friend) and *Modern Jealousy* (2022–2023). They look to me like affectionate appropriations of an ethnographic or anthropological style, which enables you to evoke the relationship between modernism and otherness.

GP The expression "natural friend" is above all my way of rethinking inter-species relationships. *L'Ami naturel* is an heteropalindrome borrowed from author Louise de Vilmorin (1902–1969), which, when spelled backward, reads "le rut animal" ("animal rutting"). I used that title for my first solo show at Tunnel Tunnel (Lausanne, 2018) and for a series of works that feature a tongue sticking out, the first instance of which was a human head facing a pig's head.

NB Your titles bring a metonymic or allegorical element to your work. *Modern Jealousy* might mean personal jealousy, but then slides closer to abstraction to become the inherent jealousy of modernity—modernity being defined as the power of abstraction—toward difference.

GP The words "modern jealousy" are spelled out by beads on overly full abacuses, where there's no room to calculate, as though the desire to count, to enumerate, to possess, has alienated the tool, and made its computing function inoperative. "Jalouser la modernité" is a cross between the feeling of envy for what we don't have and "jalousie," a type of Venetian blind or shutter that allows you to see without being seen. For that matter, the title of my show at the Kunst Halle Sankt Gallen (2023), *Moving Jealousy*, was another variation: there was a long curtain in the exhibition gallery that moved, sometimes blocking the view of certain works or access to the entrance door, at other times becoming a screen for a video piece.

NB The presence of perspectivism and nativism, the power of decolonialist discourses and commitments, and the ecological paradigm all inflect even as they fuel the cannibalistic system of contemporary culture. The times we live in reinforce the feeling that that modern narrative can no longer generate new forms.

GP Listening to you, I get these hallucinatory images of a museum collection invaded by moth, and a desert where contemporary sculptures are part of the ecosystem. Philosopher Isabelle Stengers pointed out that "the shaman and political leader Davi Kopenawa, who belongs to a people that modern anthropology has labeled 'animist,' commented that 'white people sleep a lot but dream only of themselves.'"[1]

NB The moth were disbanded, but they return through the device of a handrail. Do you view your transposed narratives as a form of return? A return of what haunts, troubles, and avenges itself on the alleged sobriety of the aesthetic gaze, of that gaze's way of using common sense to defuse the issue?

GP The handrail's function of support is fragilized and haunted—even nightmarishly—by the larval shape that imparts a tragi-comic role to the fact that the hands of the beholders unknowingly stroke a depiction of an invertebrate [p. 43]. I think the strangeness you mentioned is often present in the playful aspect of certain works, like the soup spoons dangling from wooden tongues (*L'Ami naturel I*, *II*, and *III*, 2020) and the hand-shaped turnstiles (*Drawing Holes*, 2023).

NB Yes, but there's more than humor. There's a grating, uncomfortable element, or rather an idea that things are uncomfortable, as though objects and stories convey a discrepancy or inadequacy by not quite fitting in.

GP The motorized curtain, for example (*Can't We Stop Speaking?*, 2023), has an ambiguous presence—falsely haunted, falsely functional. It has the presence of a moving object that lies or surprises, even as it thoroughly acknowledges the hoax: the motor is as visible as what it drives. The playful tone produced by this exaggerated displacement is counteracted by a certain lack of spectacle, paralyzed halfway between projection and reality, between alive and inanimate.

NB If we allow a more affective image of your work to surface, I'd say that, beyond appearances, you also manage to tease out an image of subjectivities, of solid yet thwarted, petrified, silenced groups. I'm thinking of your recent sculptures of legs capped by rocks (*Les Ombres*, 2018–2023). Something is trying to trickle out, or trying to express a feeling of being stifled. There's a lack of sound even though it squeaks—a critique of silence and the oppressiveness of art, of our situation, and our times.

GP *Les Ombres* (*Shadows*) have a grotesque appearance, they're rocks that lift their skirts and begin to walk, who seem to say, "I'm getting up and getting out of here." And yet their title alludes to a question you raised: are we looking at a statue or a mere shadow, a pretense of one? As though the work were inadequate, incapable of embodying or expressing anything. When I display representations of the body in public spaces—hands, braided hair, eyes, etc.—they are identifiable forms that perhaps allow us to split our personalities, to see ourselves as another, yet they also embody, they territorialize, or—to use an expression often employed in certain ecofeminist and decolonial struggles—they rethink things from the standpoint of body-as-territory.[2] By linking the body to its surrounding environment, this notion also weaves the individual body into the collective body. Maybe the idea of community can be found in this gathering

1
Isabelle Stengers, "Et après? De quoi notre héritage nous rend-il capable ?" in Jean Birnbaum (ed.), *Hériter, et après?*, Gallimard, Paris 2017, p. 143, quoting Davi Kopenawa in Bruce Albert and Davi Kopenawa, *Chute du ciel. Paroles d'un chaman Yanomani*, Terre humaine, Paris 2010, p. 284, published in English as Bruce Albert and Davi Kopenawa, *The Falling Sky*, trans. Nicholas Elliott and Alison Dundy, Belknap Press, Cambridge, Massachusetts 2013.

2
See Mara Montanaro, "Genèse d'une catégorie d'analyse et d'une méthode de lutte : le corps-territoire," in *Théories féministes voyageuses : Internationalismes et coalitions depuis les luttes latino-américaines*, Éditions Divergences, Paris 2023, p. 153–224.

of rocks with skirts, in the group of gargoyles sticking out their tongues, and in the modes of production of these objects that pass through various hands.

NB You find ways of resisting not only the apolitical tendency of the lone art object, but also the complacency of art that recounts narratives with political import. As though you managed to defuse one through the other. You never abandon the issue of art, its meaning and its potential, but rather address it through the difficulty of reconciling procedures and institutions with the narratives and collective practices that trigger art. Thus, alongside pleasure, there is also an open, generous conversation with difficulty, negativity, and impossibility.

Patron/Partner, 2022 →
Moving Jealousy, Kunst Halle Sankt Gallen, St. Gallen, 2023 → →

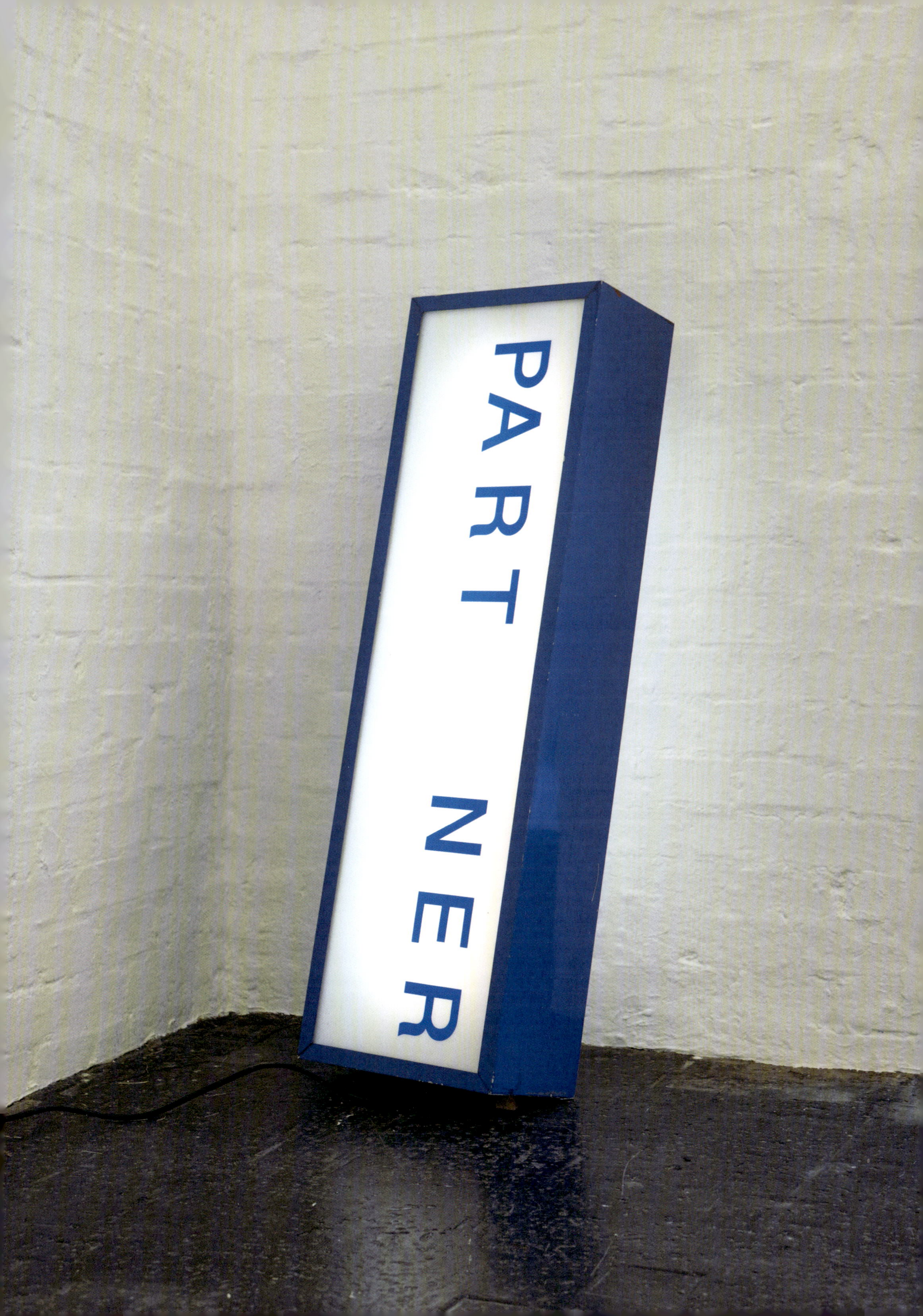
PART
NER

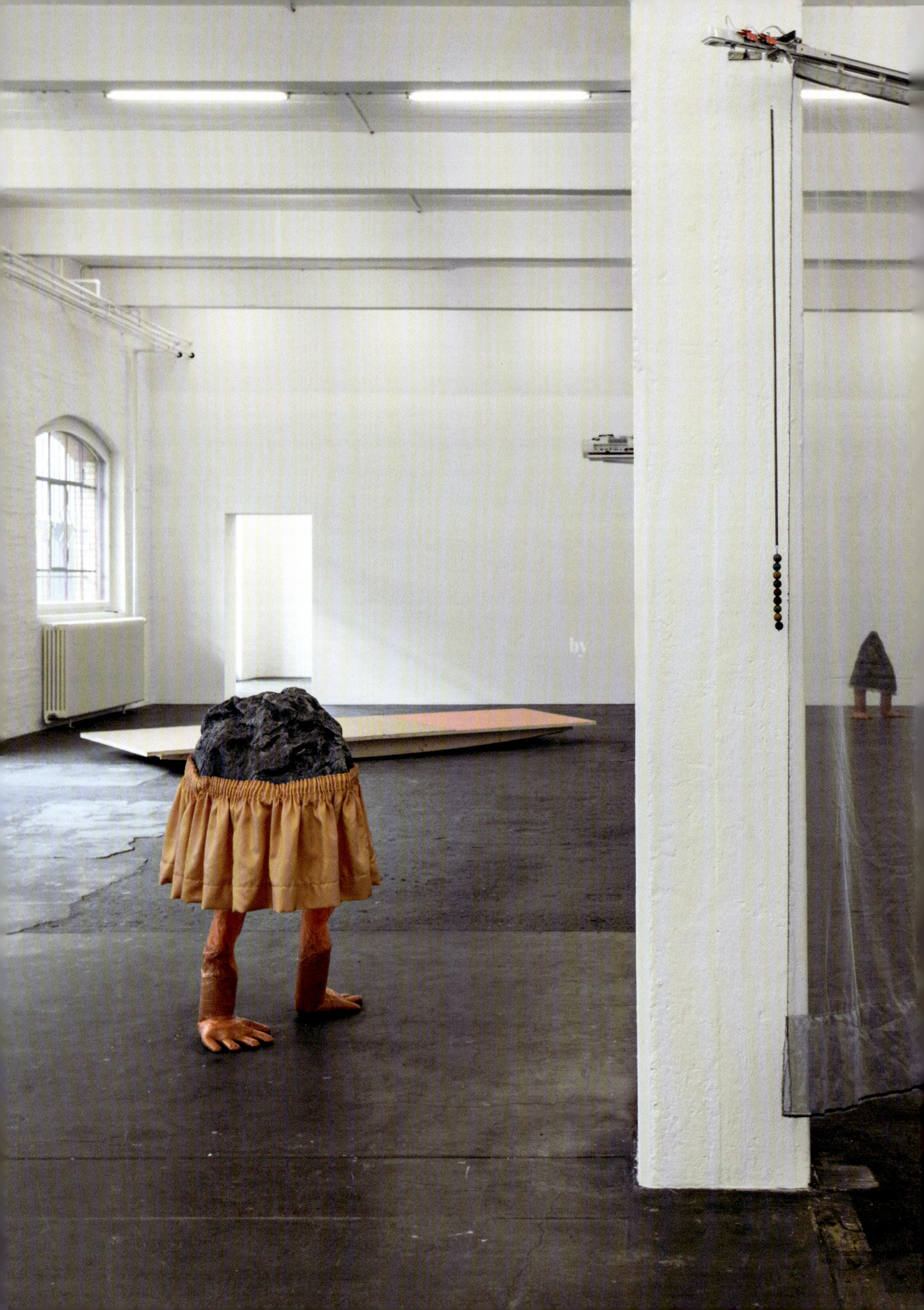

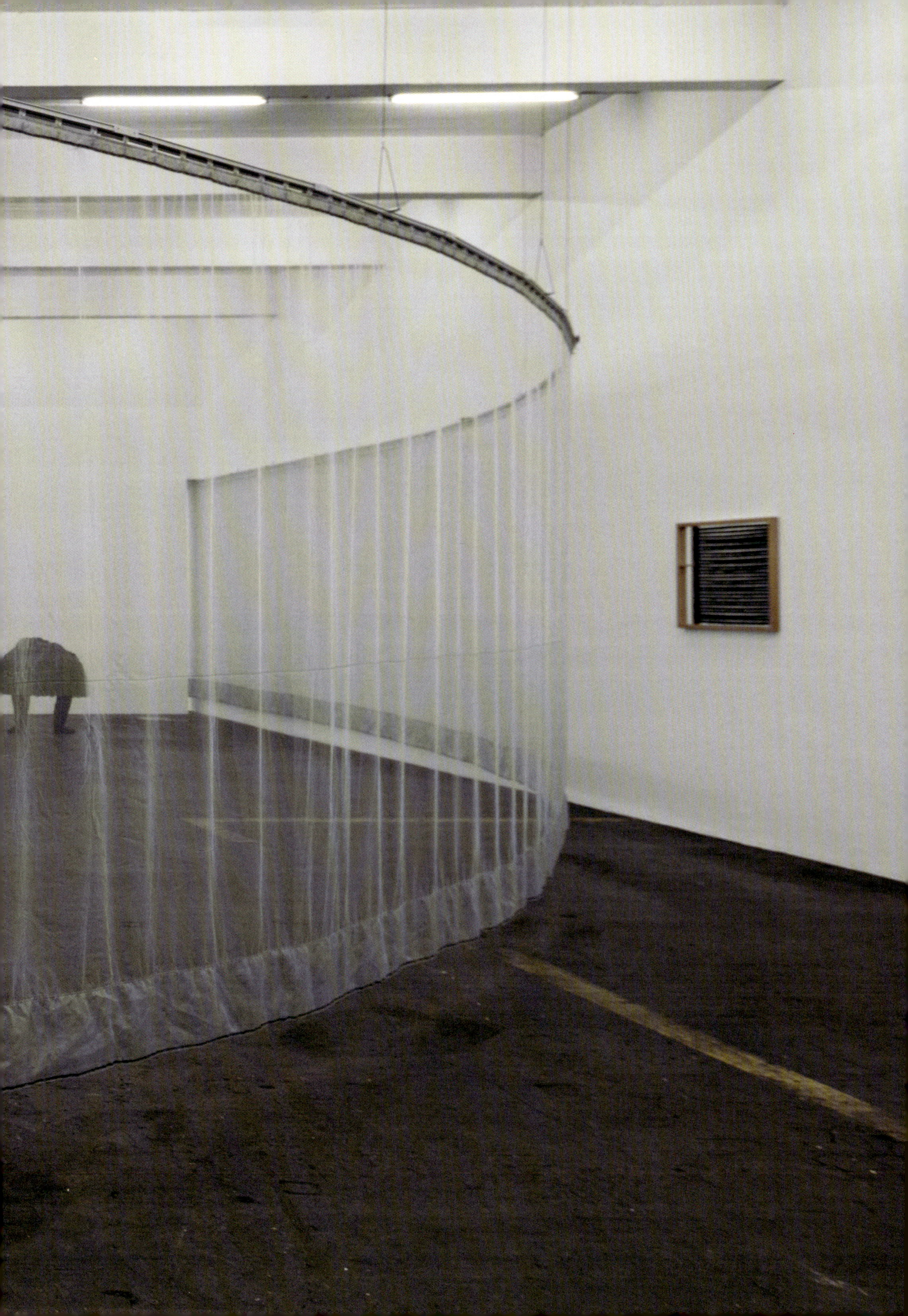

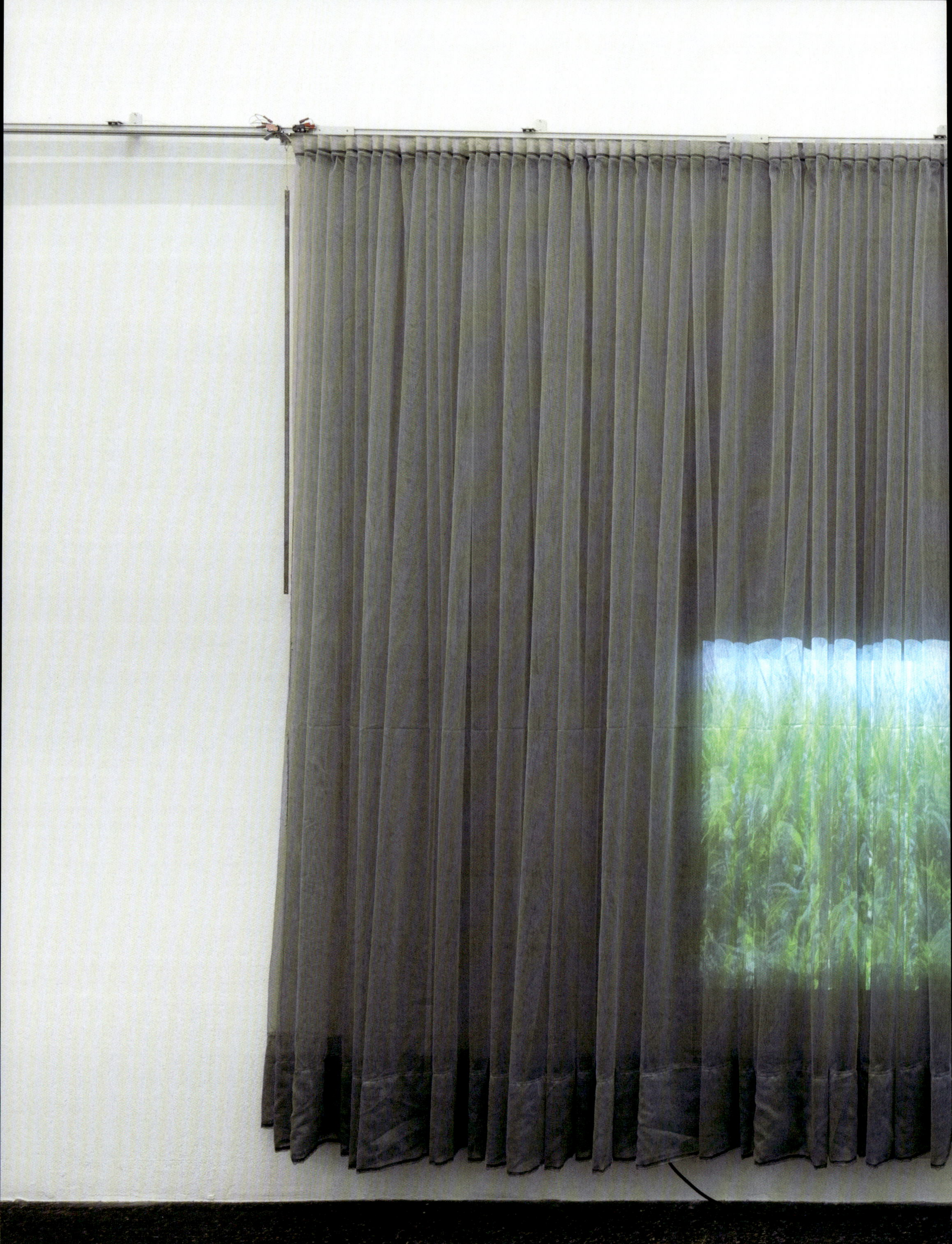

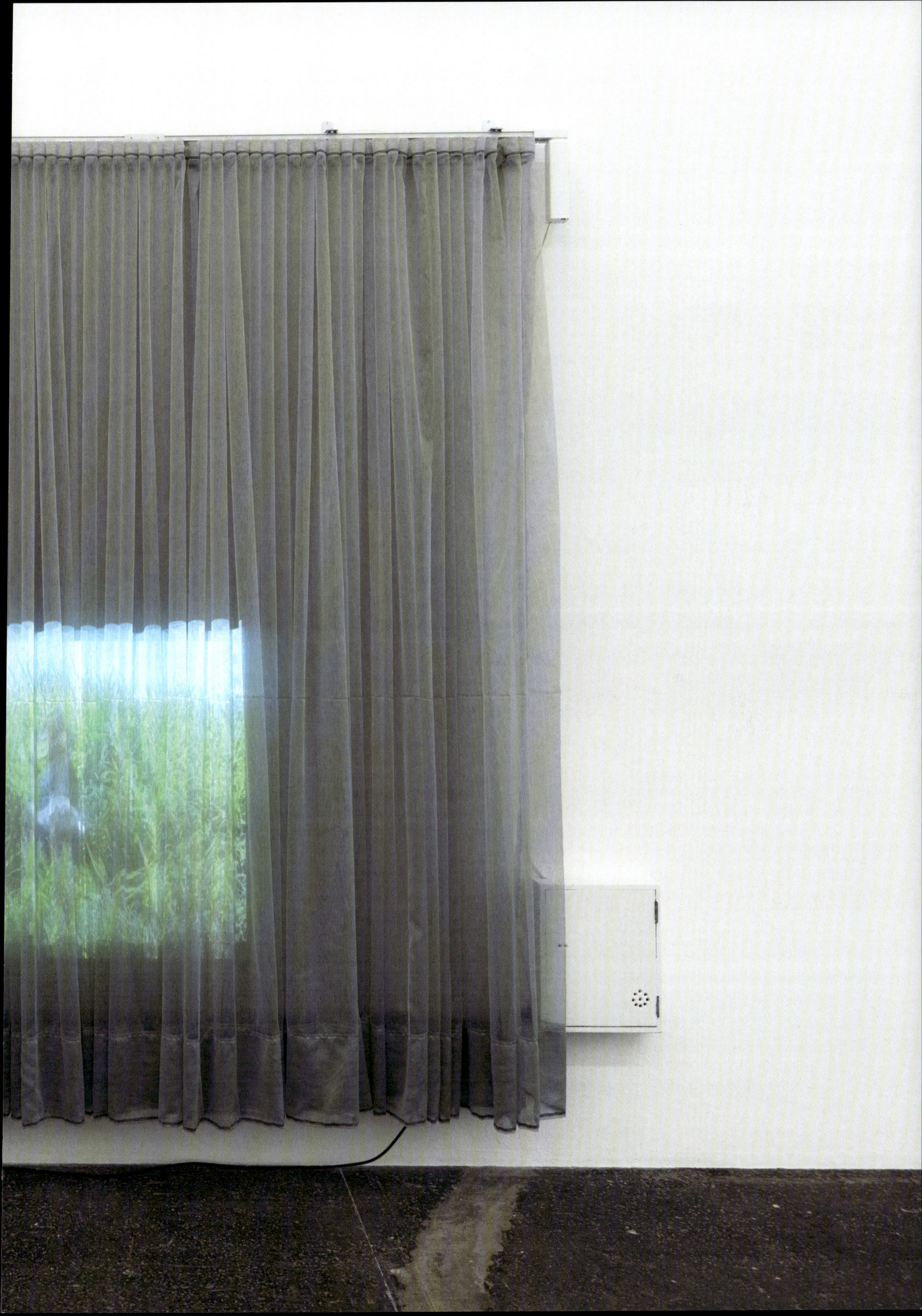

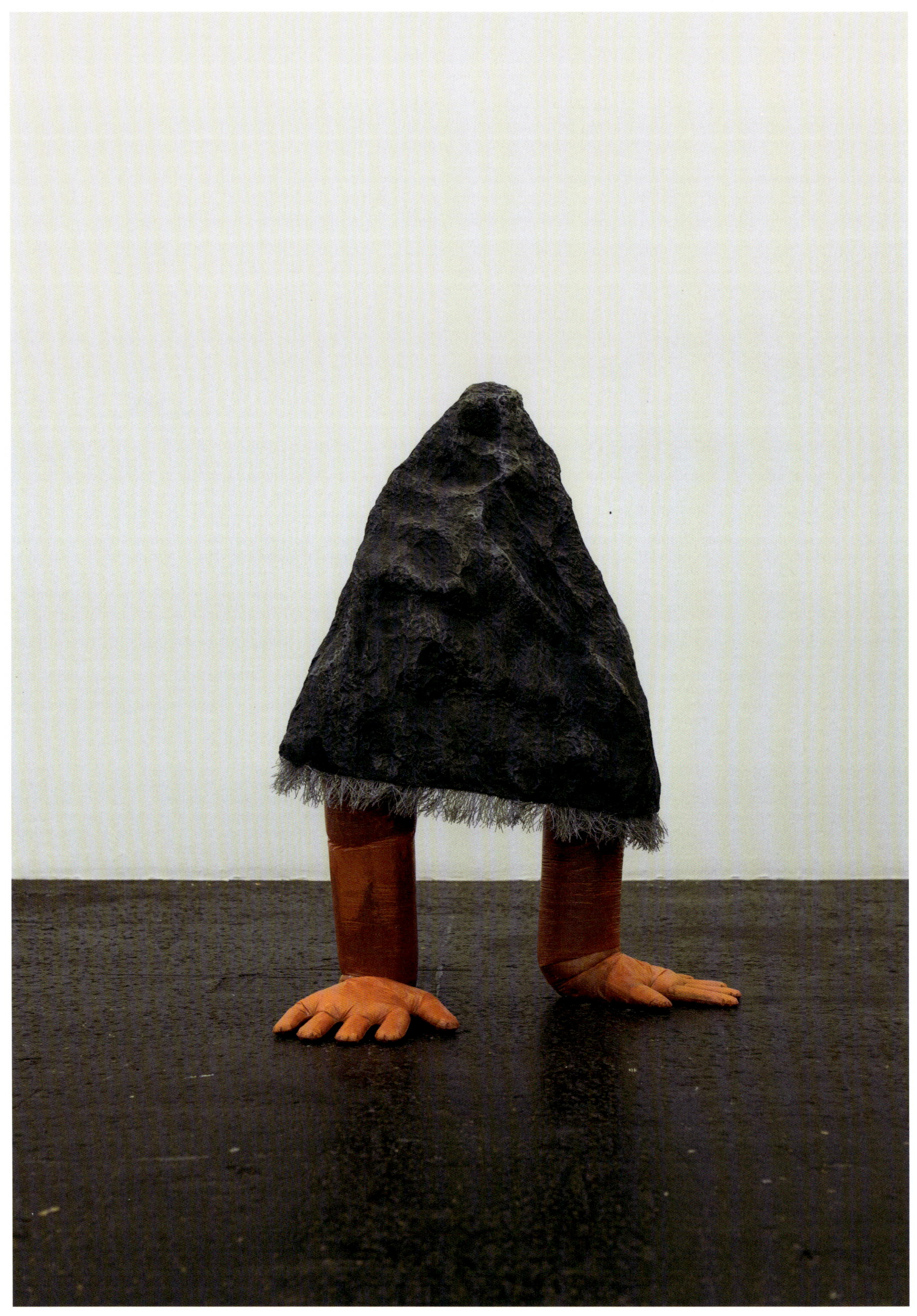

Shadow I, 2023
← *Can't We Stop Speaking?*, 2023

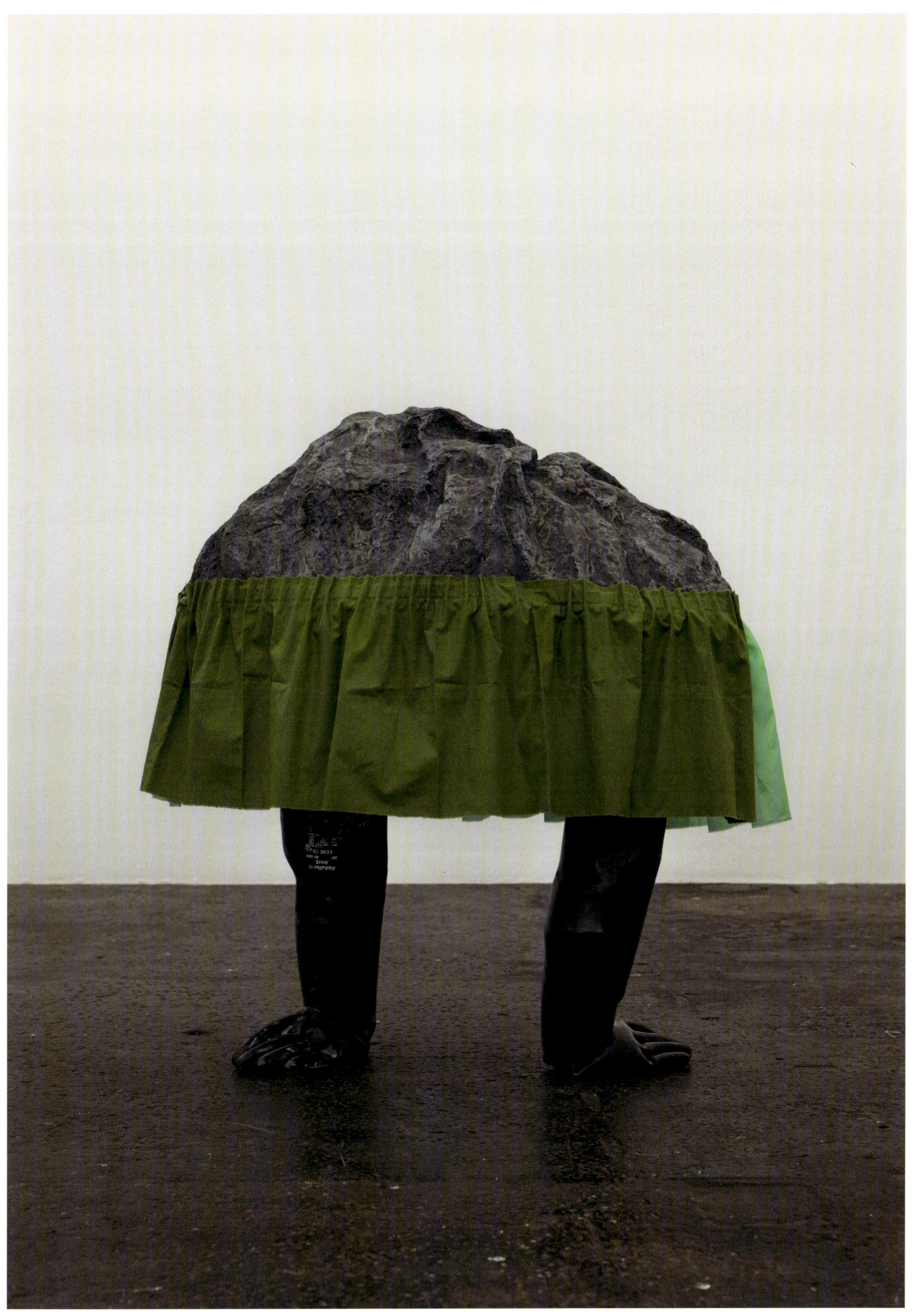

Shadow II, 2023

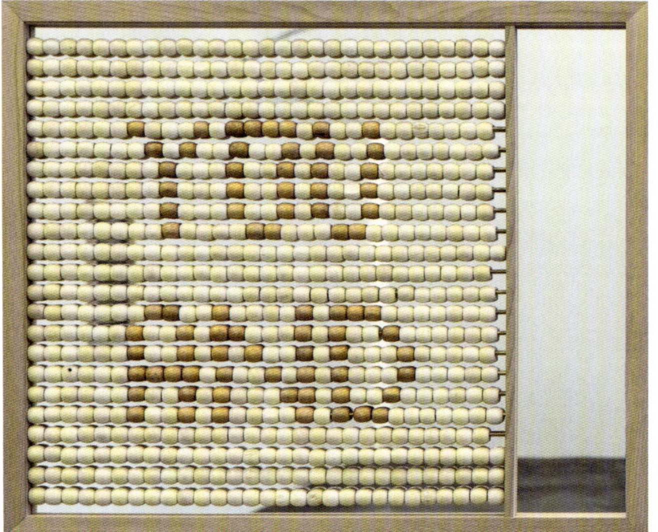

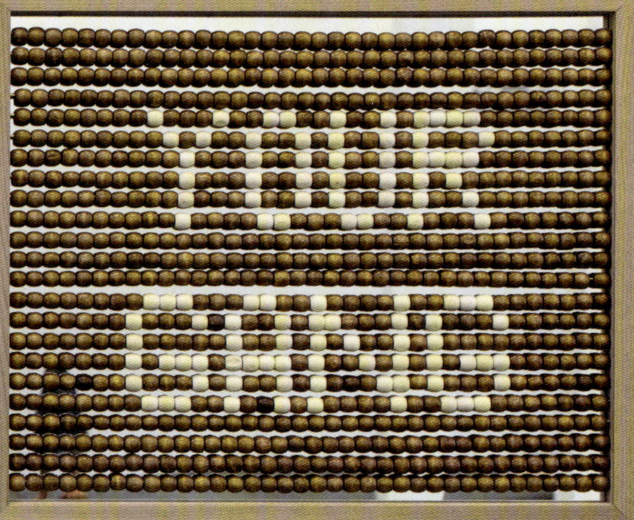

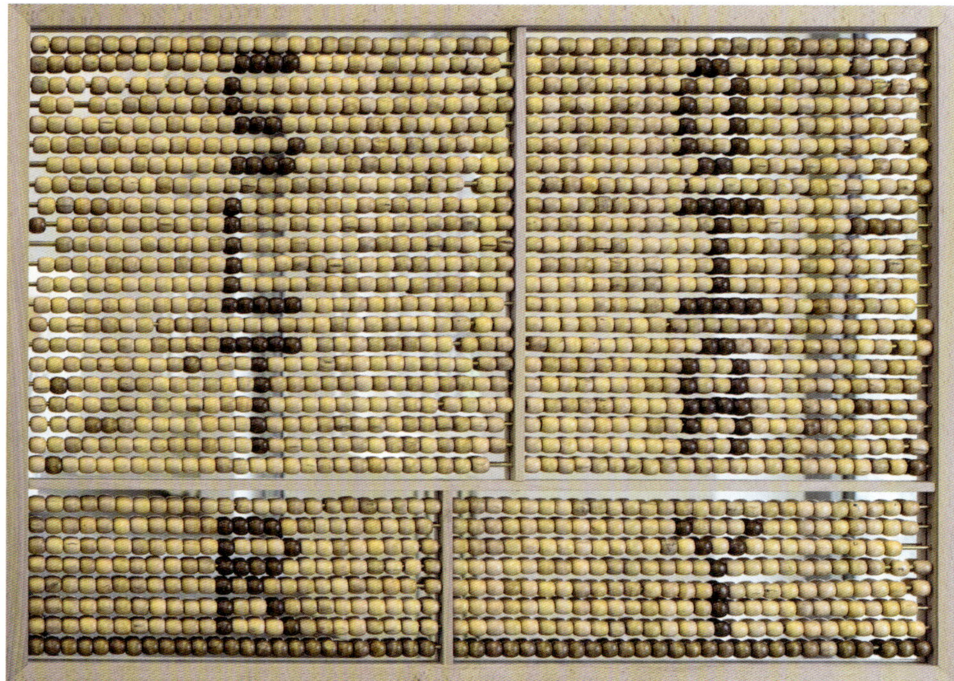

You and/Your Gang, 2023
Solitary/Solidarity, 2023

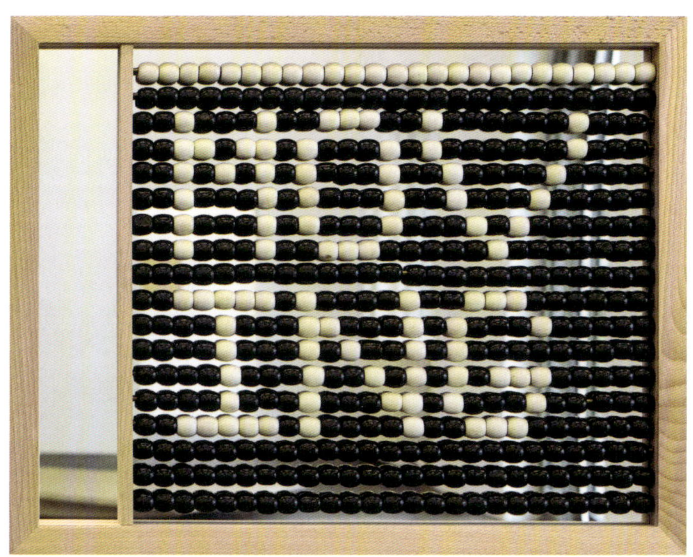

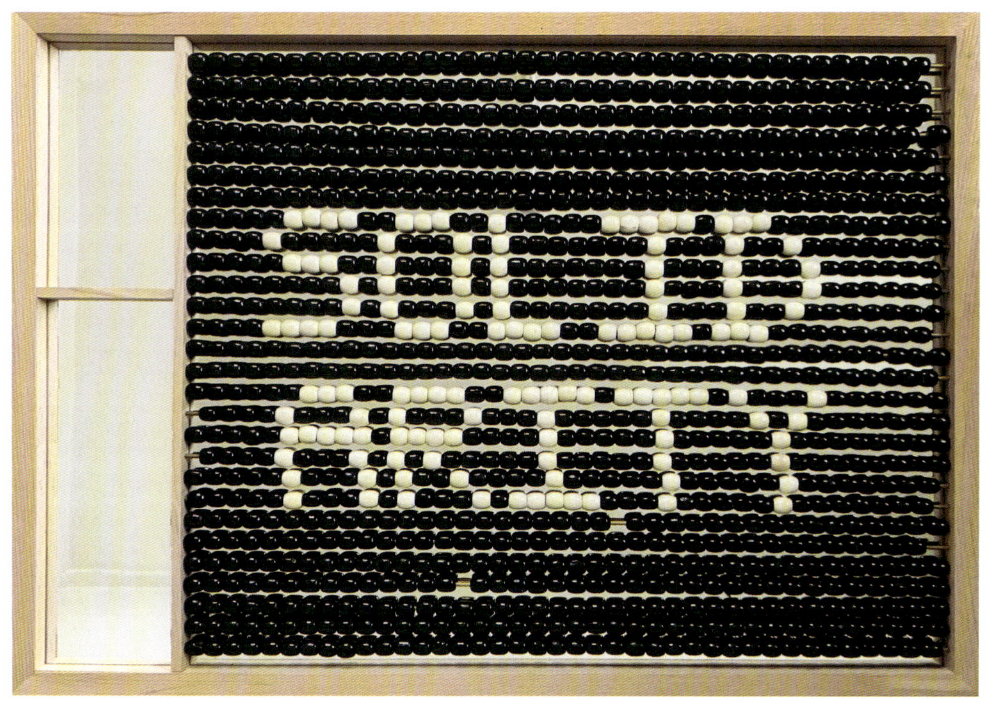

Moving, 2023
Solidarity/Solitary, 2023
Dormant Season, 2023 →

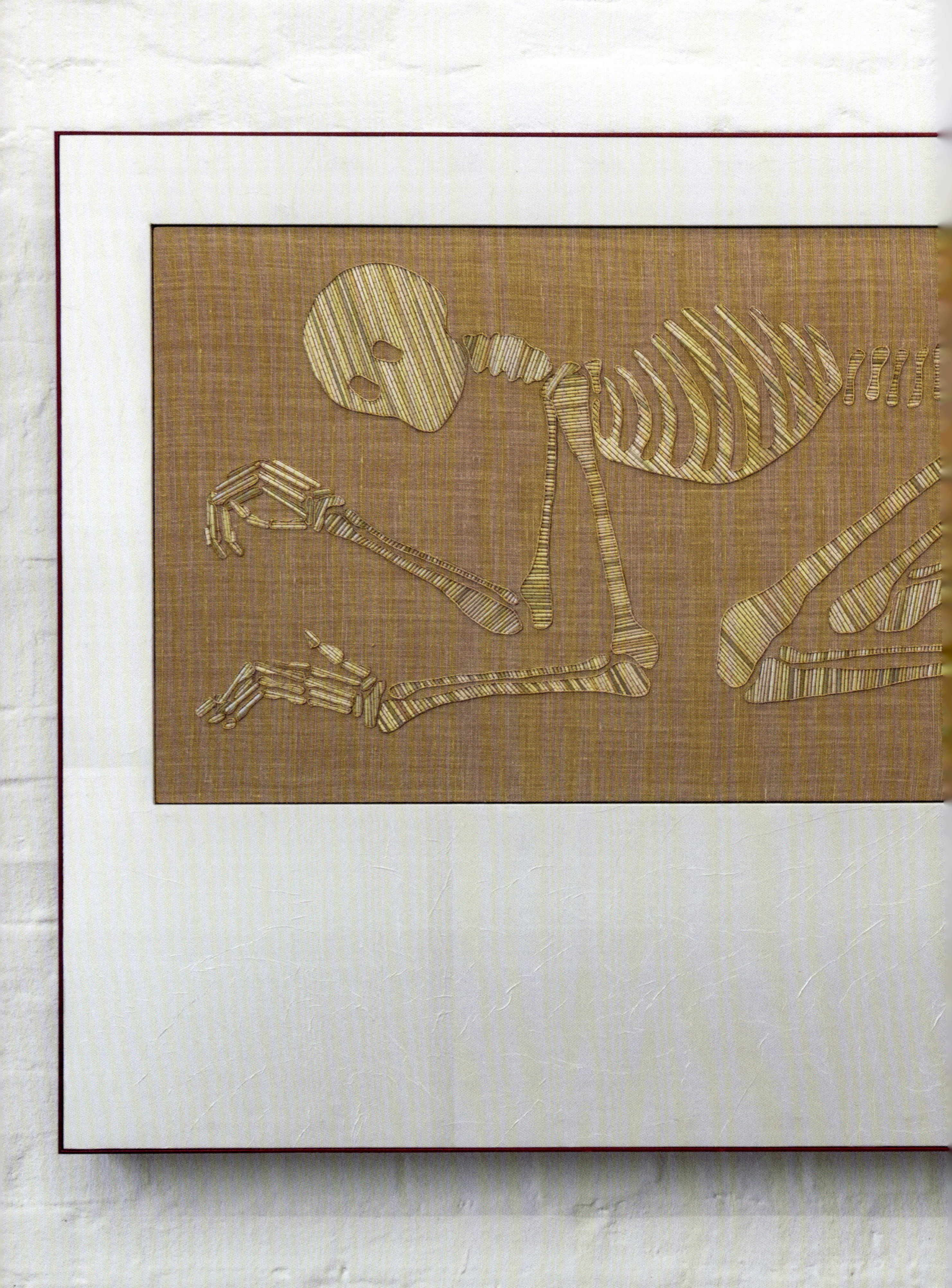

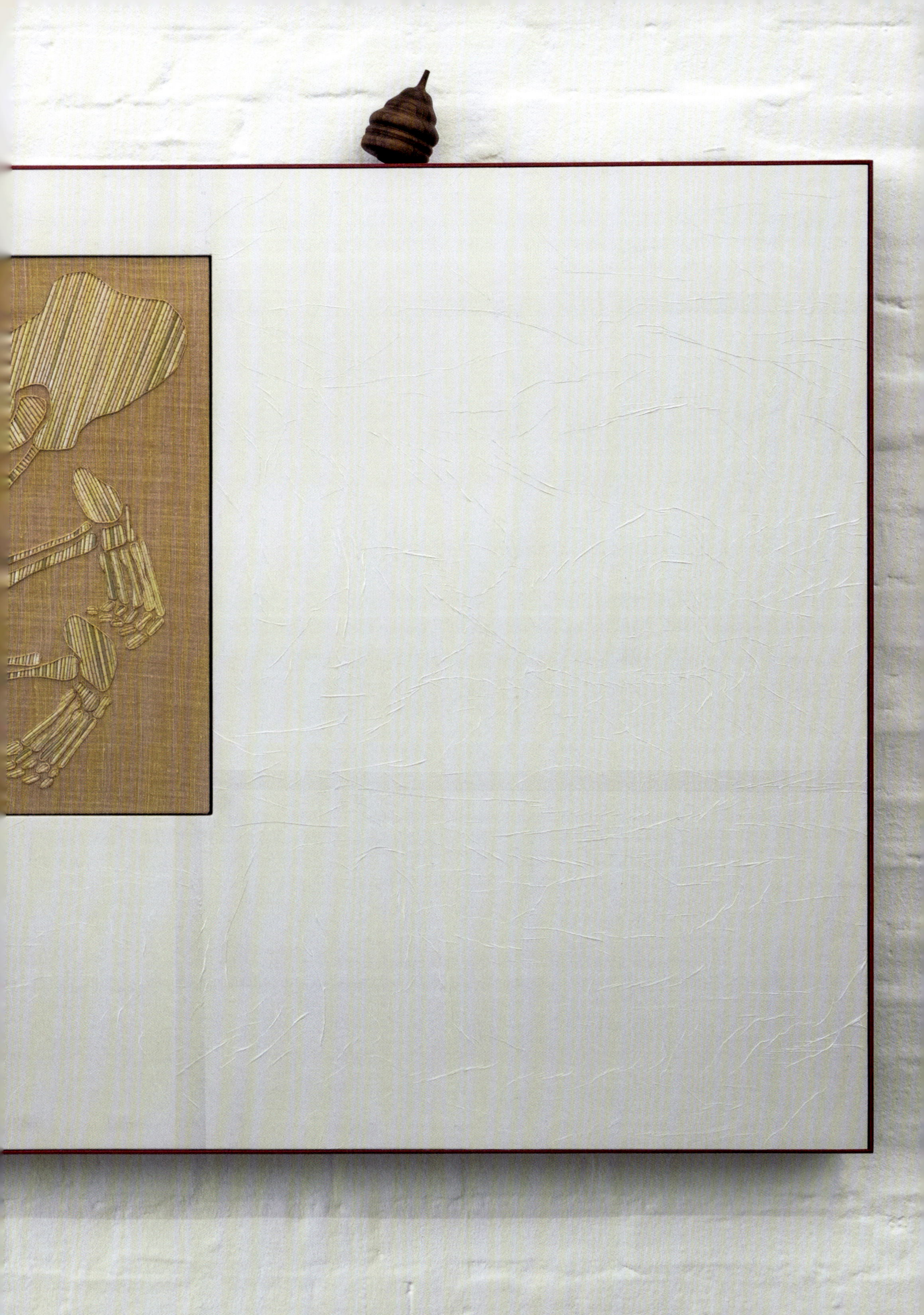

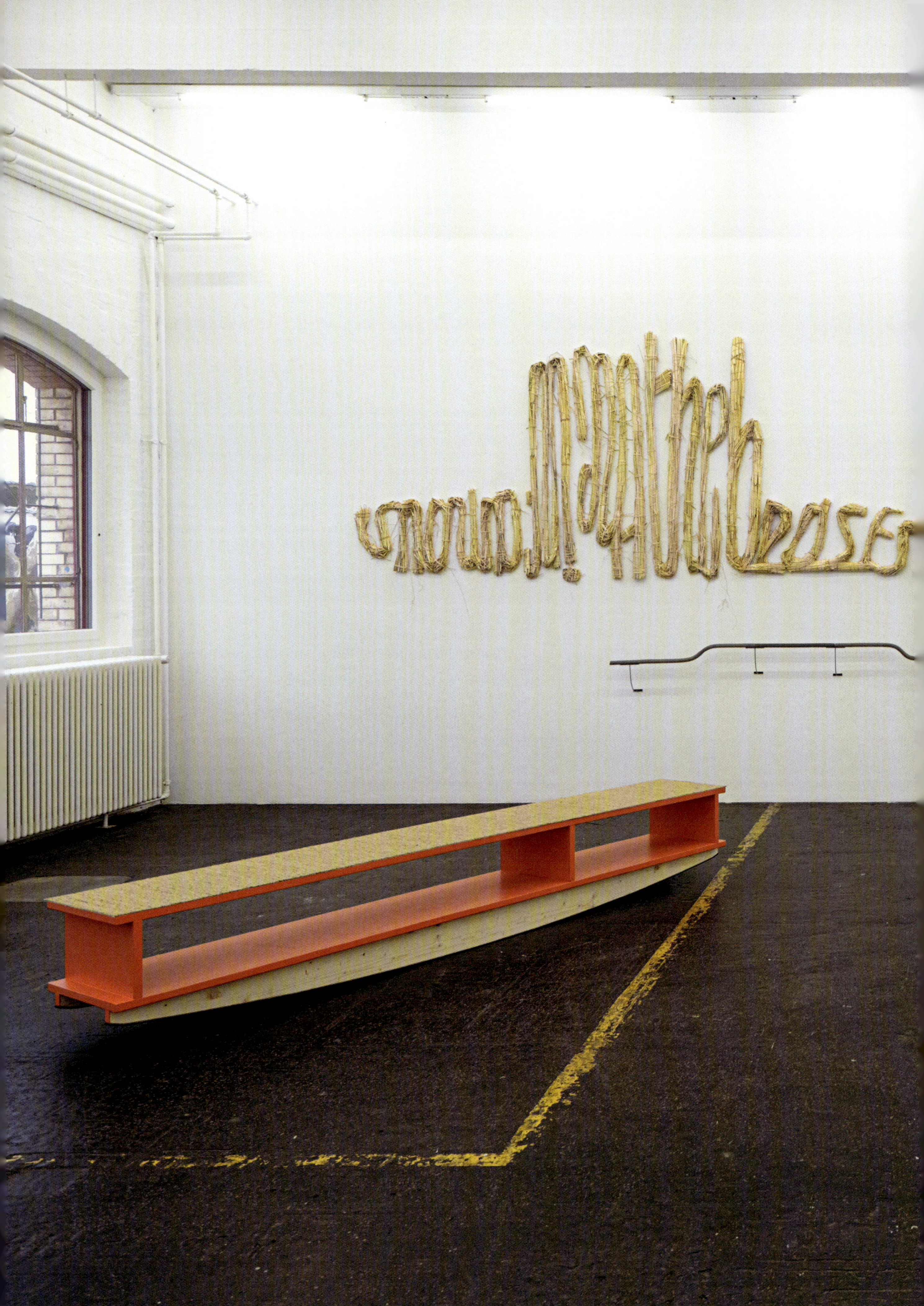

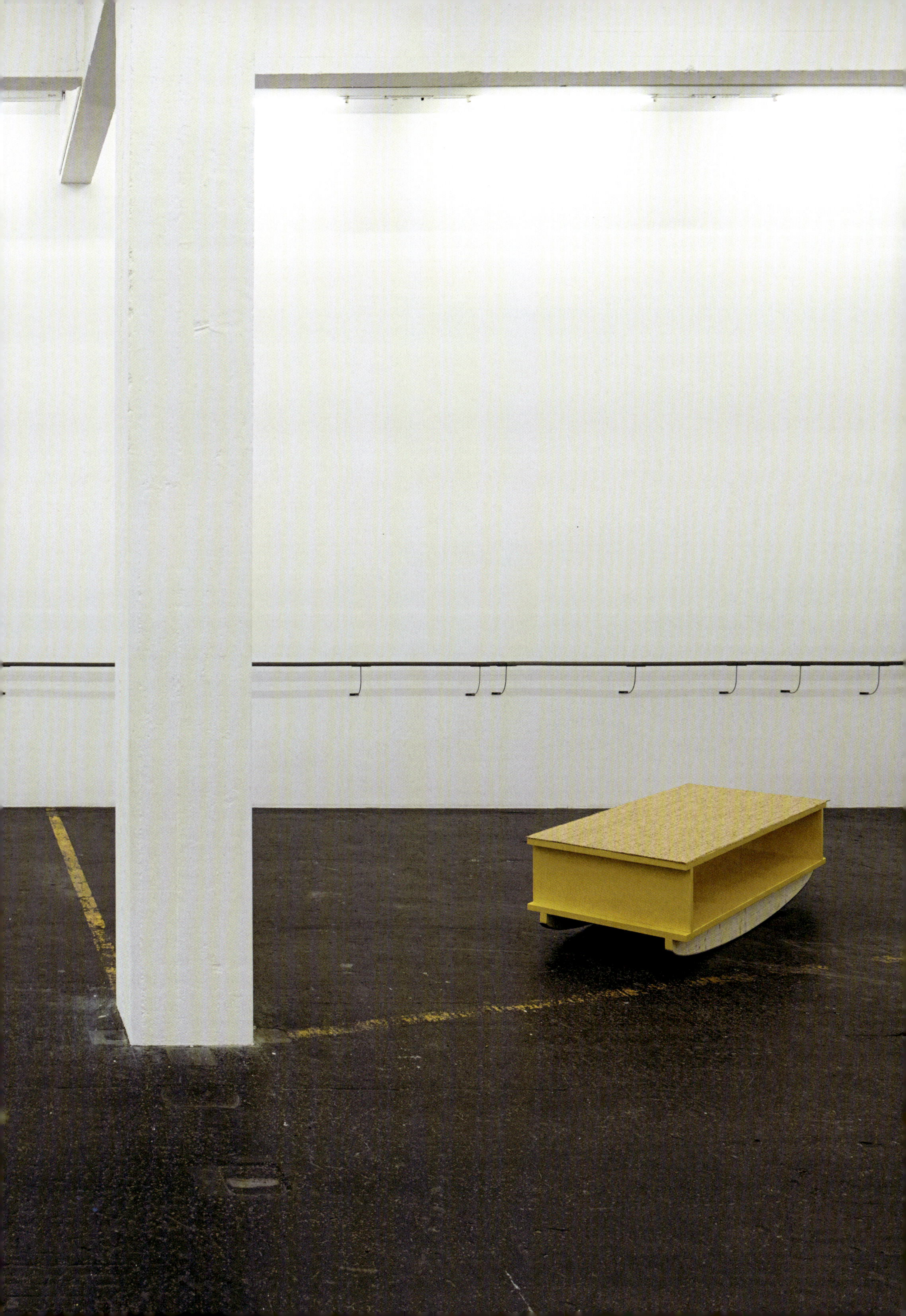

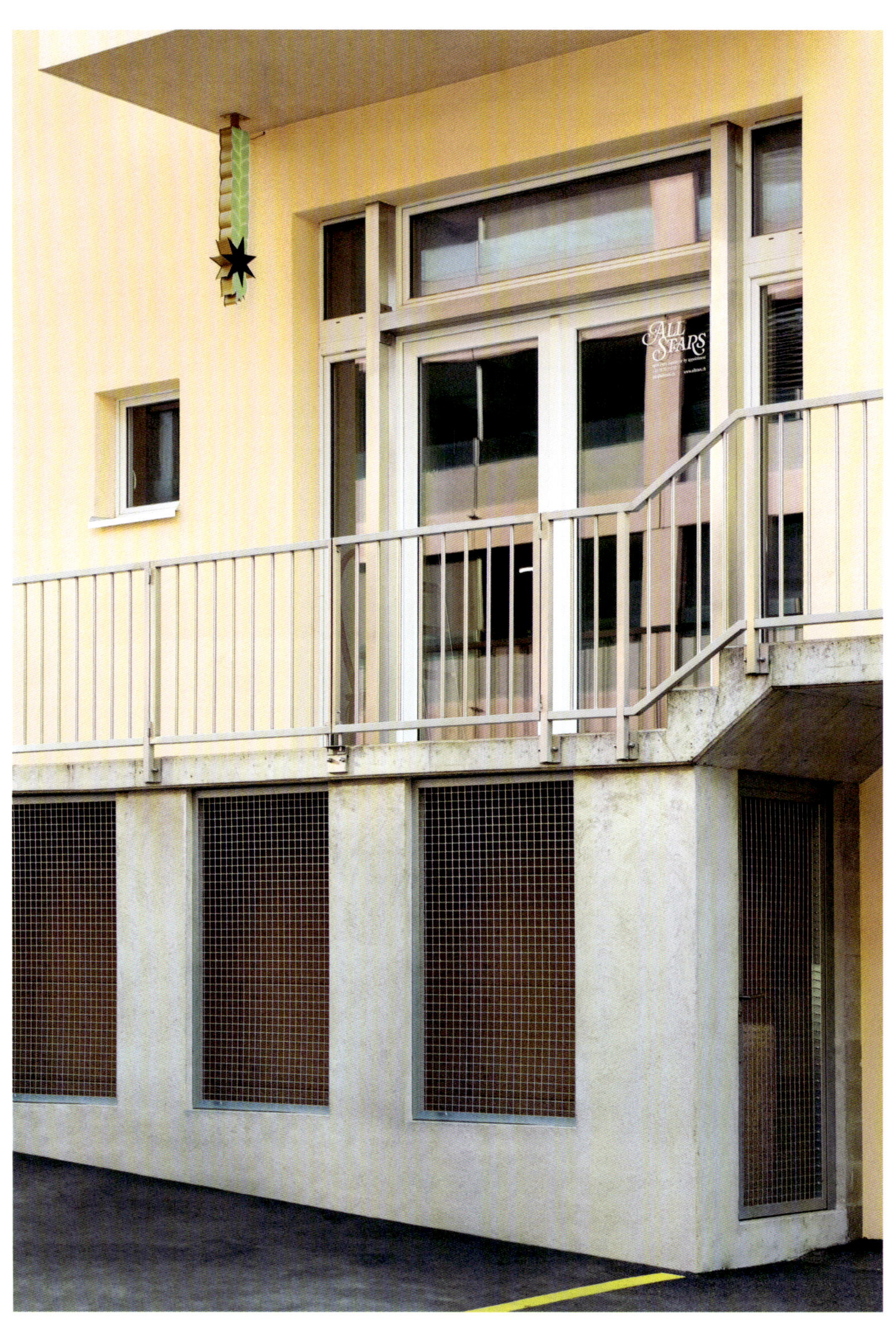

Auto-confiance, 2021
← *Moving Jealousy*, Kunst Halle Sankt Gallen, St. Gallen, 2023

Catch a Falling Star

Sabrina Tarasoff

From time immemorial, many have marveled at the enigmatic appearance of a star falling through the sky, taking the transience of the experience, in its swift and luminous passage, as a pretext for everything from political prophecy to poetic trope. From the meteoric omens that moved classical etiologies, to Walt Disney's heart-felt wishfulness, the falling star—"a 'dead letter' even in classical times,"[1] as folklore scholars Hilary Belcher and Erica Swale remind us—carries meaning in its imaginative leap. As an enduring, fixed image in motion, it models the tropical element in all discourse; the bright flight intimates change, turning events, and pending outcomes, as much as it illuminates our desires. Remiss to miss what is at stake; namely, the *tropic*, from the Greek "tropos," for "turn": a measure of change marking shifts in meaning. "Tropic is the shadow from which all realistic discourse tries to flee,"[2] writes historian Hayden White, suggesting that our tendency to resort to metaphorical language is a constitutive element of all discursive reason. In its sudden descent, the star appears from the penumbra of figurative meaning to alight on what logic cannot preside over: the void left behind, the visible gap, the arresting silence. The star's departure from eternity entices questions such as what returns to us, in what form, and to what end?

Similar questions underwrite Gina Proenza's artistic practice, as vested in the *re*-figuration of imaginative hypotheses on what returns to us from the void, the invisible, what escapes emptiness, or logical expression. Consider her a collector of proverbial meteors: stories, events, and expressions, which seem to have descended into a contemporary formal syntax from gaps left on historical record. Ambiguous meaning contorts in time, and so finds formal currency. According to Mark S. Lussier, writing on vortices in William Blake's poem *Milton* (1804–1810), the falling star, in its sudden emergence from the distant reaches of outer space to a poetic present, also suggests "a correspondence or complementarity between perceptual and physical processes."[3] John Milton, for example, describes the sun setting over his *Paradise Lost* (1667) as "dropt from the Zenith like a falling star"[4]: a simple line, which Blake would later revise in his poem on Milton, to describe his perception of the poets'

1
Hilary Belcher and Erica Swale, "Catch a Falling Star," *Folklore*, London, vol. 95, no. 2 (1984), p. 210.

2
Hayden White, *Tropics of Discourse: Essays in Cultural Criticism*, The Johns Hopkins University Press, Baltimore 1997, p. 2.

3
Mark S. Lussier, *Romantic Dynamics: The Poetics of Physicality*, Palgrave Macmillan, London 2000, p. 91.

4
Thomas H. Luxon (ed.), *The John Milton Reading Room*, available on https://milton.host.dartmouth.edu/reading_room/contents/text.shtml, last accessed April 2024.

cosmic relation. "I saw him in the Zenith as a falling star," Blake re-visions, "descending perpendicular, swift as the swallow or swift;/And on my left foot falling on the tarsus, enterd there."[5] While Milton employs the metaphor to describe the physical action of a cosmological event, Blake's Milton-star drops *ex nihilo* from the void only to land on, and then move *into* Blake's left foot. The star tunnels through poetic space-time to make literal their poetic convergence as a single shape.

5
William Blake, *Milton: A Poem in Two Parts. The Complete Poetry and Prose of William Blake, 1804–1810*; available on https://blake.lib.asu.edu/html/milton.html, last accessed April 2024.

Examining colloquial expressions against formal records, across various modes of visual production, Proenza draws our focus to semantic convergences closely akin to Blake's transformative and convoluted poetic continuum. For Proenza, this marks a concern with moments when our language falls short of logic, and we are moved to search for alternate modes of expression. Communicative devices, game tokens, and objects crack open communications across epistemological boundaries. Signs fall short of their own meaning. Speaking, moving parts, like mouths, feet, and legs, lose the context of their whole. Allusions to stages, sets, and platforms suggest something of the theatricality of knowledge production. Placards are lost for words, left with nothing but scrambled vowels, and perplexing cues. In other words, the works come to resemble and resound what is lost in historical translation, as an ongoing process weaving folklore, social life, and affective politics into the larger project of intellectual reason. As a result, Proenza's works often assume the shape of things stuck mid-transition. While boulders, wax feet, or abacuses register an interest in historical time frames, Proenza's scene-setting nevertheless happens within contemporary art's formal lexicon. Her recombination of recognizable and unfamiliar motifs alike both register and resist conventional modes of interpretation. Proenza understands that meaning tends to "slip away from our data toward the structures of consciousness with which we are trying to grasp them," writes White.[6] Like so, the mechanics of transformation underwrite the artist's discursive logic; her works descend from the shadow of meaning to alight on differential expression.

6
Hayden White, *Tropics of Discourse: Essays in Cultural Criticism*, p. 1.

Consider all illumined under Proenza's *Auto-confiance* (2021): a glowing, single braid, "descending perpendicular" from the ceiling outside All Stars' independent art space in Lausanne. Held together with a seven-pointed, star-shaped hair tie, the LED-sign shines light on semantic signification. To contextualize, the piece was commissioned by the space as a permanent fixture, and so intended to site-specifically reflect on the collectivity and exchange present in the local scene. In this sense, Proenza's gesture was almost challenged forth by Friedrich Schlegel's prompt that "a dialogue is a chain or garland of fragments. An exchange of letters is a dialogue on a larger scale, and memoirs constitute a system of fragments. But as yet no genre exists that is fragmentary both in form and content."[7]

Employing Romantic strategies of extraction, compression, and recombination, Proenza's star-braid falls into a continuum with artistic

7
Jörg Heiser, "A Romantic Measure," Ellen Seifermann and Christine Kintisch (ed.), *Romantischer Konzeptualismus/Romantic Conceptualism*, Kunsthalle Nürnberg and BAWAG Foundation, Nuremburg and Vienna 2007, p. 139.

practices and theories, wherein an emphasis is placed less on singular masterpieces than on the discursive opportunities they might create. Her star-braid professes its titular "confidence" in art's tropological capacities, especially through shared encounters and at multiple vantages. The glowing sign is a guiding light in semantic darkness. As a physical object, it simply directs the gaze to its expressive language, as the site that enables its interpretive framework. Proenza's *Auto-confiance* shines a light on semantic convolution as a fact of any sign-language. Clearly, the sign articulates her commitment to site-specific reception, in its belief in daisy-chained exchanges made possible in art making, and moreover defines the boundary conditions that impel her practice. Clinging to the braid, the star is emblematic of her work's larger attempt to tie histories of language, social experience, and local politics into the moment in which these processes collapse into form.

This is certainly true of the falling star, but also of other motifs throughout her practice: tongues, spin tops, and semi-closed mouths; rocks with feet, abacuses, light boxes, each perhaps echoing what Anne Carson once wrote about mythic heroines, who, when touched by tragedy, have "left behind human form and rational speech and yet have not let go the making of meaning."[8] Pervasive allusions to motion point us in the direction of change, as forced forth in time. Ideas are formed, fall into abstraction, and still find ways to speak. Proenza puts forth the loss of proper articulation as a necessary condition: words are lost in the works' expressive momentum. Mechanical works, things rotating on motors, wind, hands and mouths in motion, motion-sensors, counting devices, and emotional valences charge the practice with a sense of semantic instability. Some meaning is always lost in the emotional errancy of the exchange, which fixates the viewer's attention on the storied practice of taking us somewhere, being *moved*. Words are turned into visuals; colloquialisms into formal document; and feelings fixed as fact.

Proenza's visual narrative comes to resemble the paratactic morphing of fairy tales, in which the tale only ever unfolds in the partial or complete absence of the conjunctive clause. Fairy tales, as Ludwig Wittgenstein would suggest, also do not speak, but generate narrative through units of impression, as a language of visible elements: tongues, worms, falling stars. These visual units, when placed in sequence, come to form "internal relations," as remarked by Wittgenstein in a side note to the 1918 draft of the *Tractatus*: "Like the two youths in the fairy tale, their two horses, and their lilies. They are all in a certain sense one."[9]

Proenza stages a similar intuition about what happens when, as Wittgenstein later writes, language "goes on holiday"[10]; the loosening of language future-shifts. Even in the partial absence of causal logic, Proenza's fragments manage to exert influence on one another. That is, rational failure tends to fall into a reliance on figurative value. Meaning is

8
Sophocles, *Electra*, trans. and annotated by Anne Carson, Oxford University Press, Oxford 2001, p. 44.

9
Colin Radford, "Wittgenstein and 'Fairy Tales,'" *Marvels & Tales*, Boulder, Colorado, vol. 2, no. 2 (12–1988), p. 106.

10
Ludwig Wittgenstein, *Philosophical Investigations*, trans. G. E. M. Anscombe, Blackwell, Oxford 1967, p. 19.

always trying to escape its own limits. Proenza, in pointing to such dynamics, gravitates to reversals in meaning, which one imagines —*falsely*—makes language recede in order to reveal something inside, according to common ideas about what renders us "speechless." Proenza's chosen subjects remain in the awe-inspired moment of being lost for words at the sight of something outside ourselves. In this, her sculptures come across as a nomenclature of the transient lapse. These are forms of ruptured cohesion, subjectivity. The artist seems to suggest that we pay closer attention to the dynamic actions underwriting aesthetic processes, rather than their final forms and fixed expressions. The line of flight reifies as personal destiny.

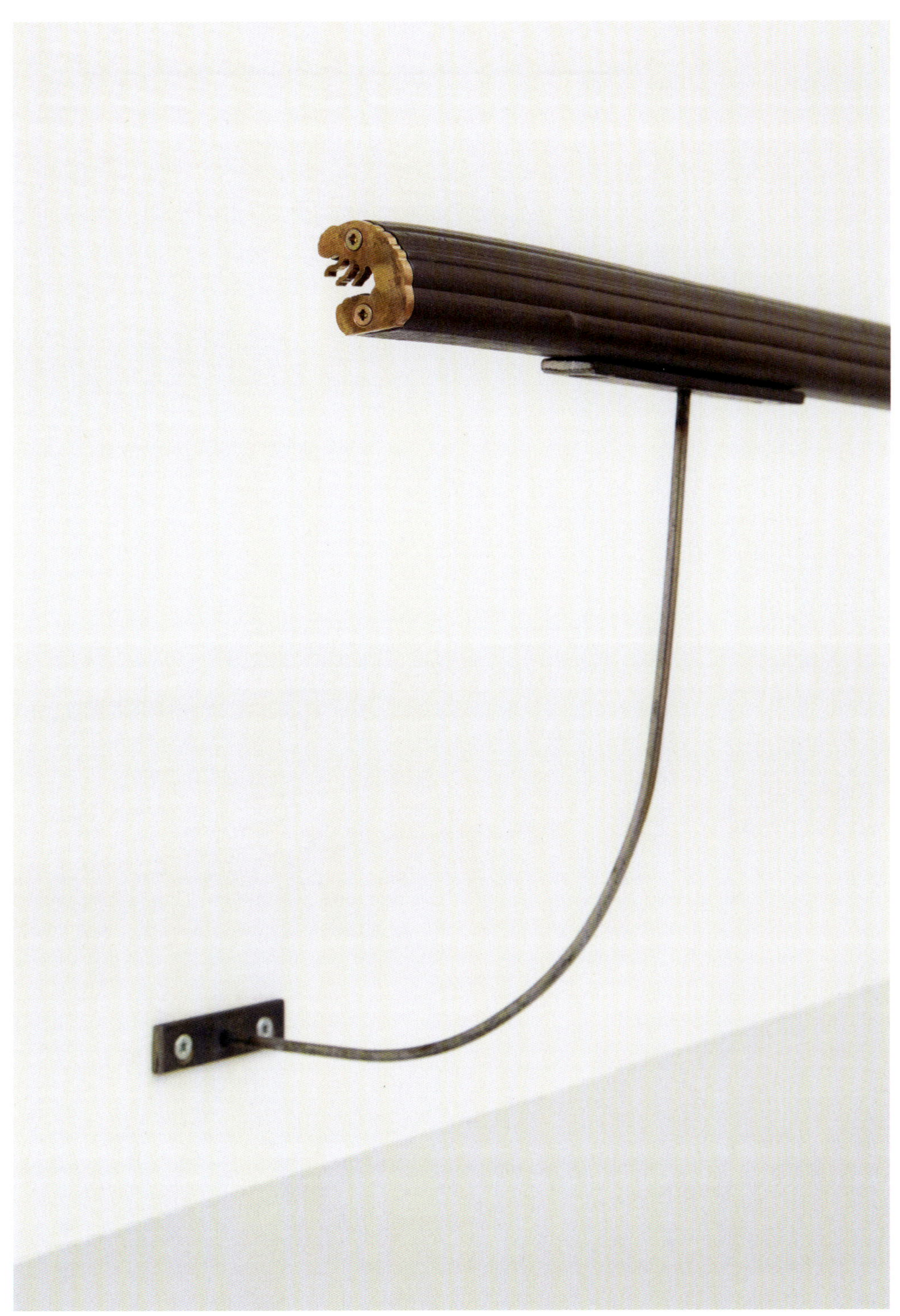

Main courante, 2023
Toi et ta bande, 2023 →

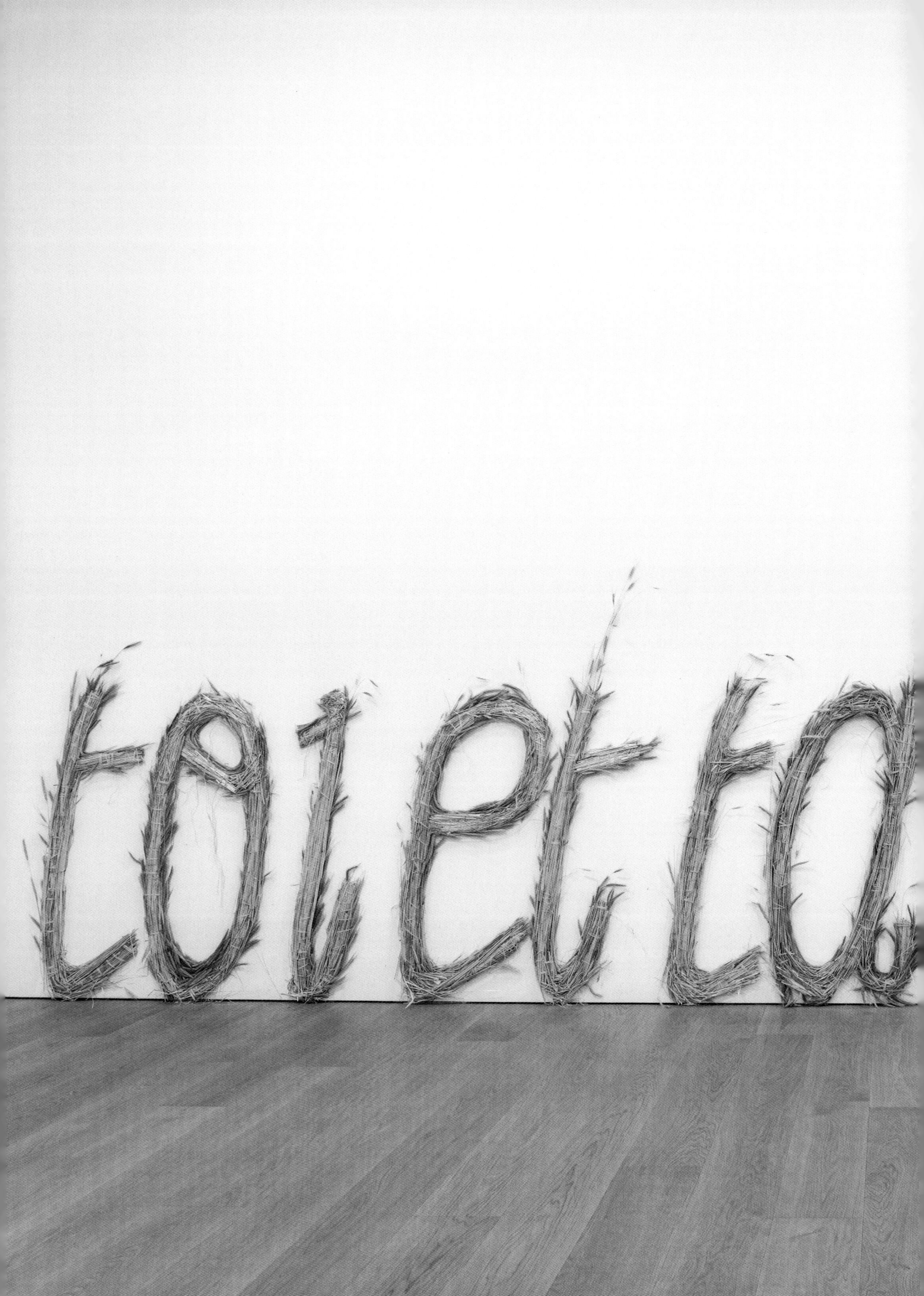

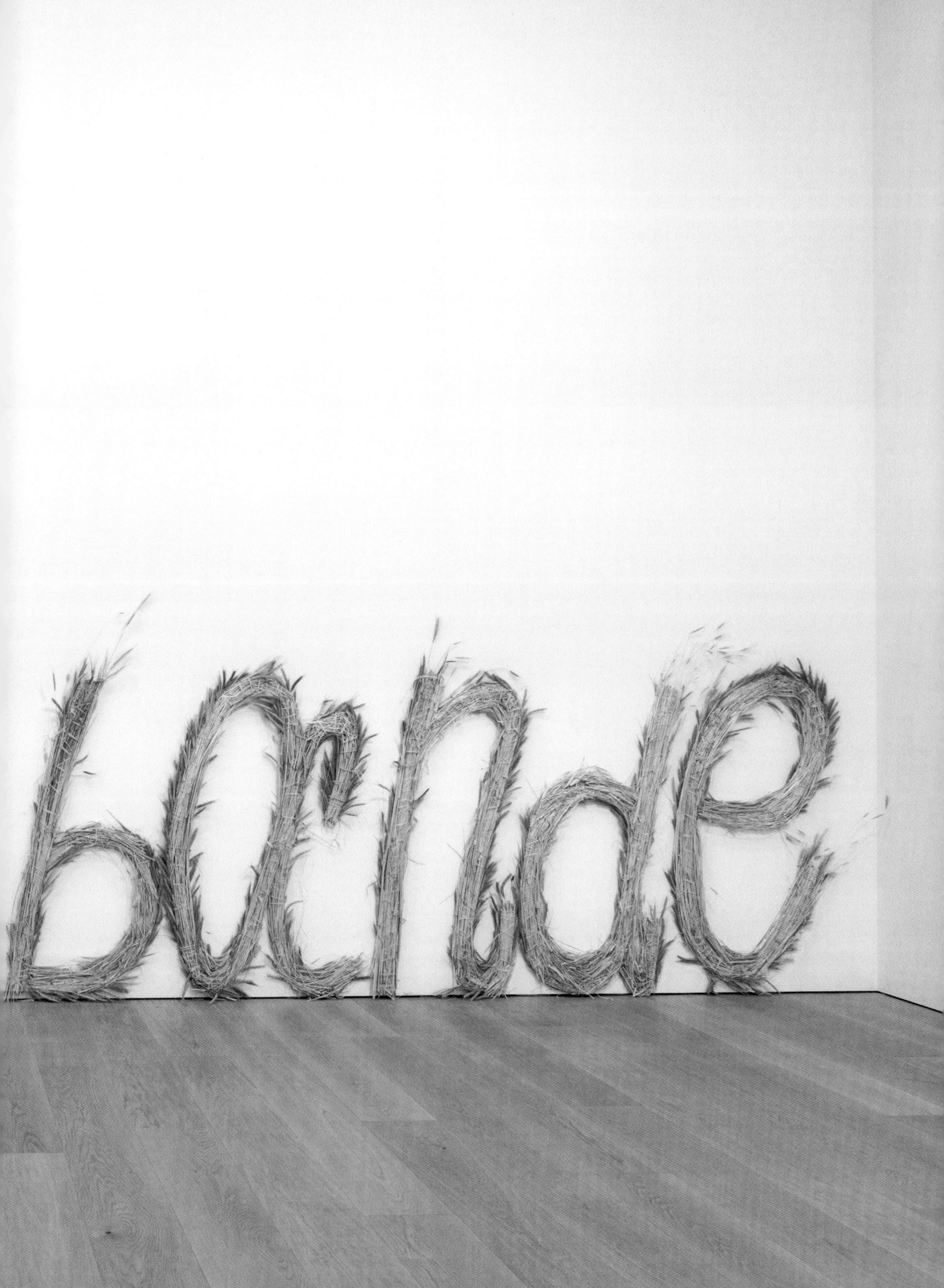

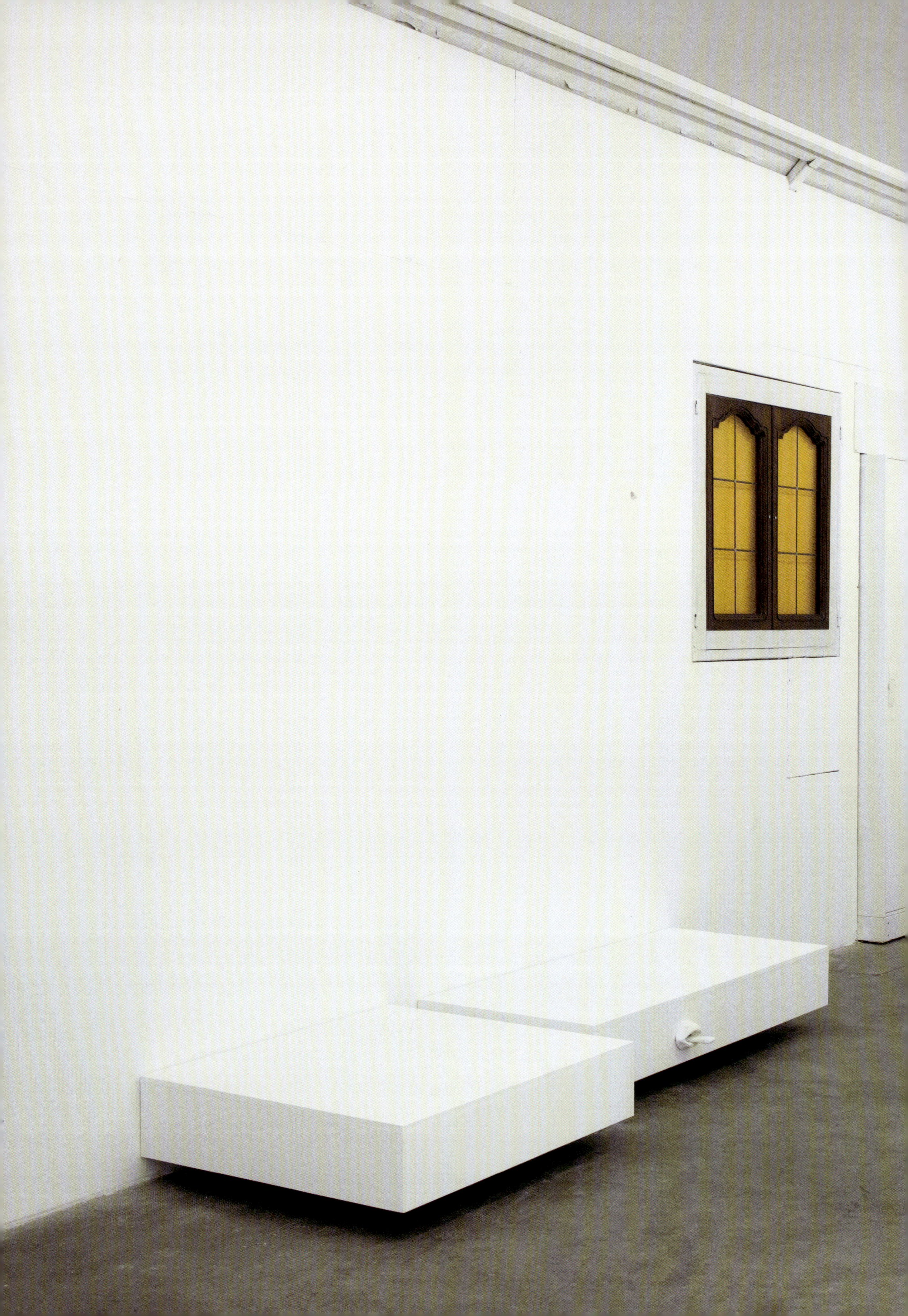

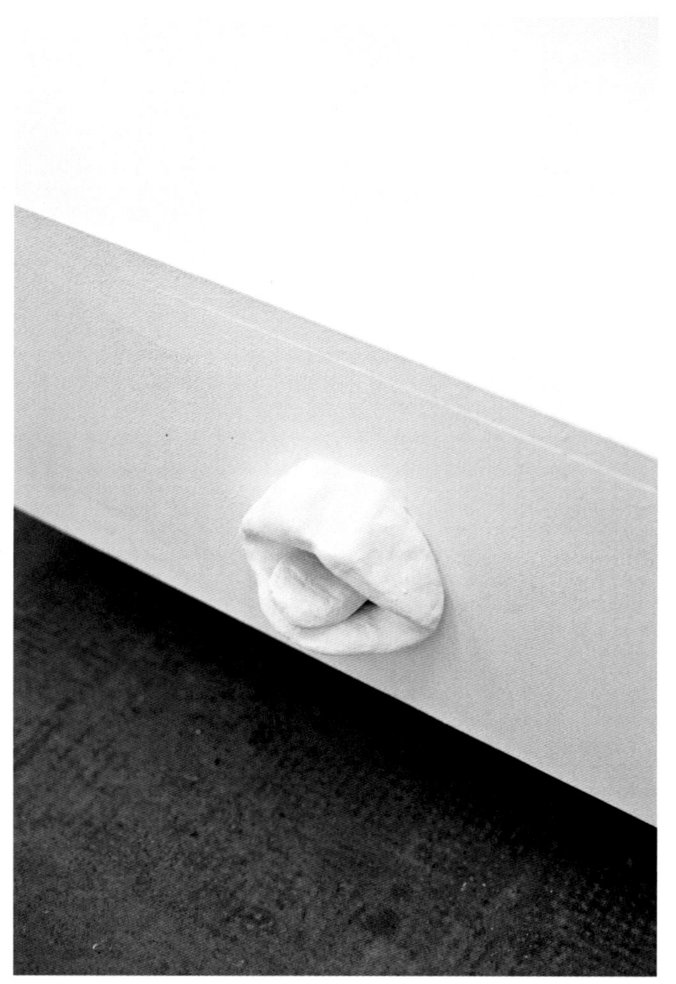

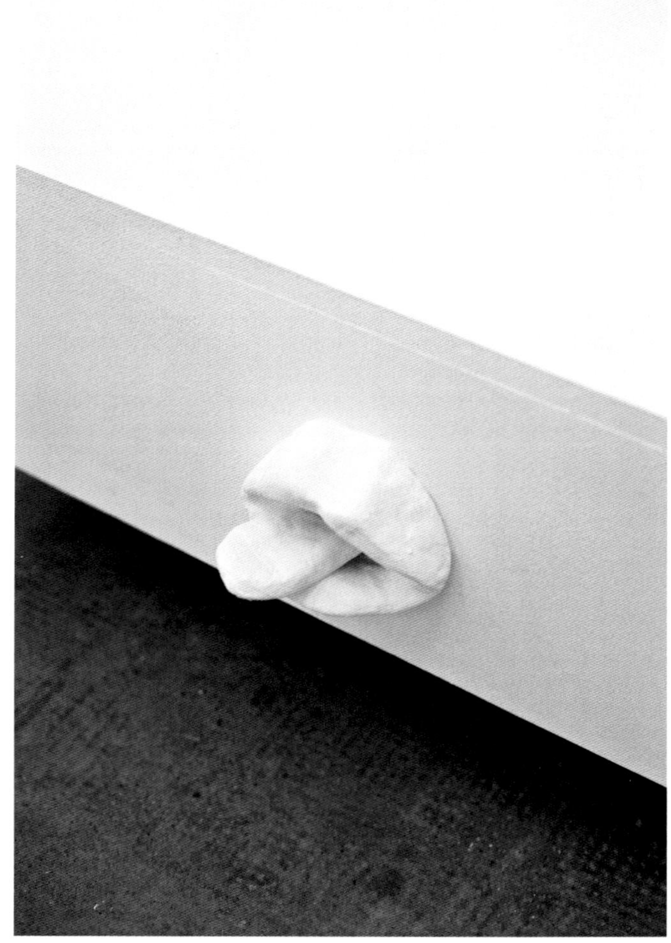

Le Rut animal II, 2018
← *L'Ami naturel*, Tunnel Tunnel, Lausanne, 2018

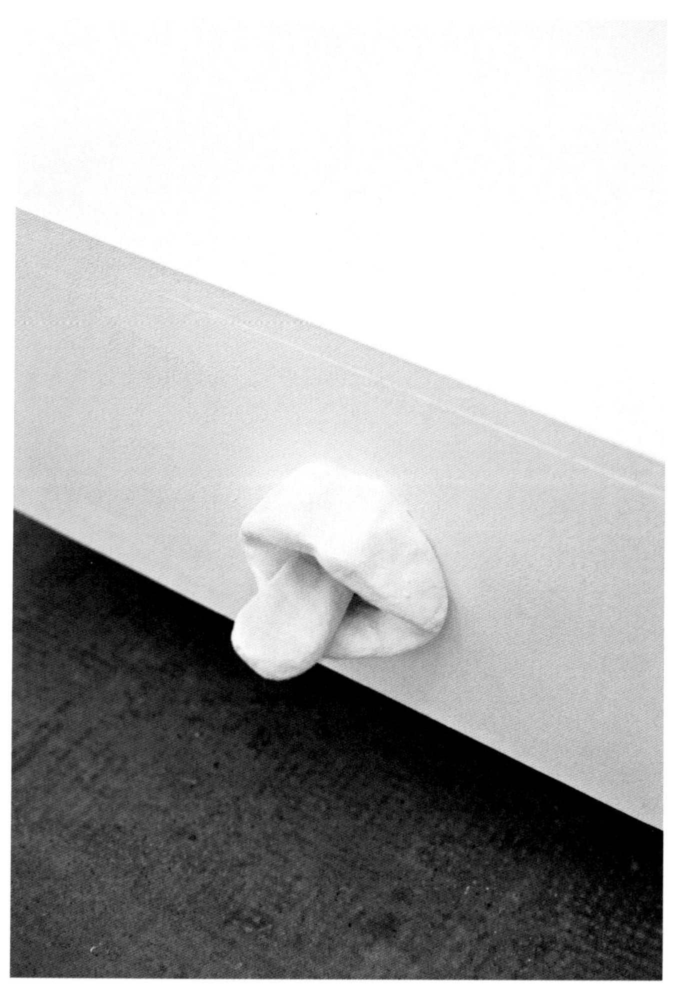

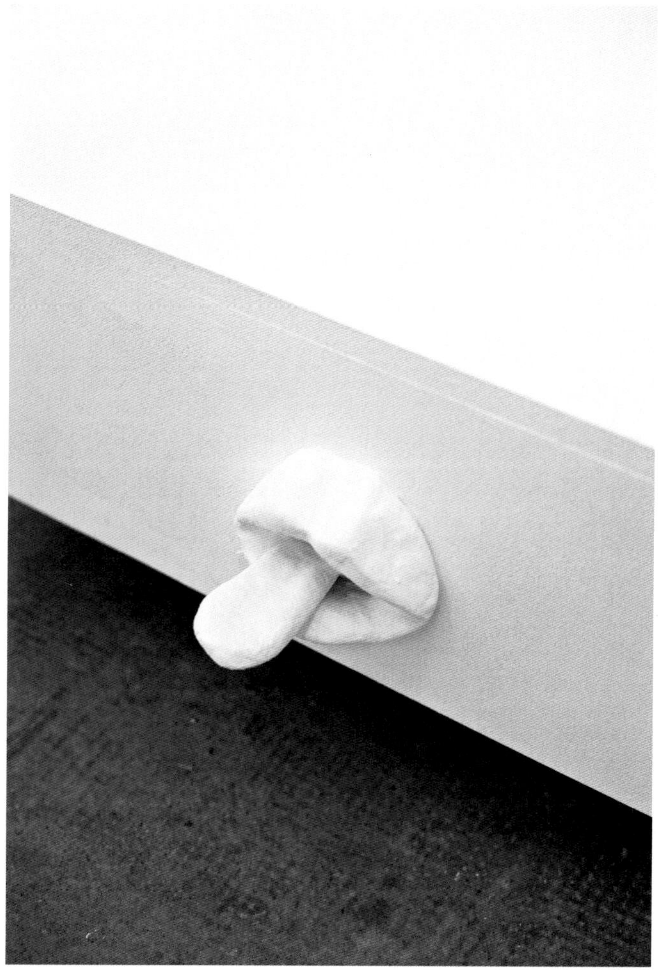

Rassemblées (Suto), 2018 →

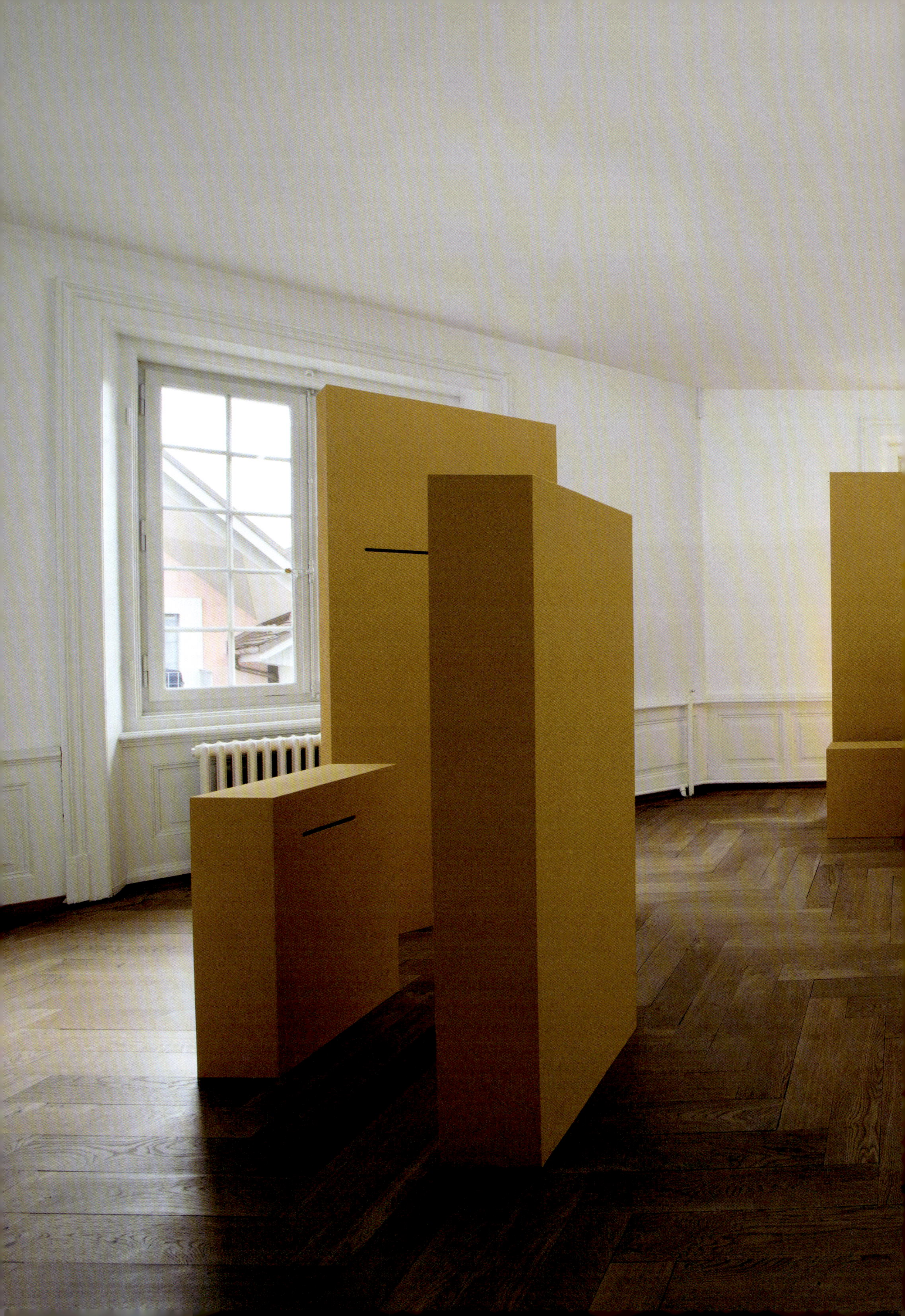

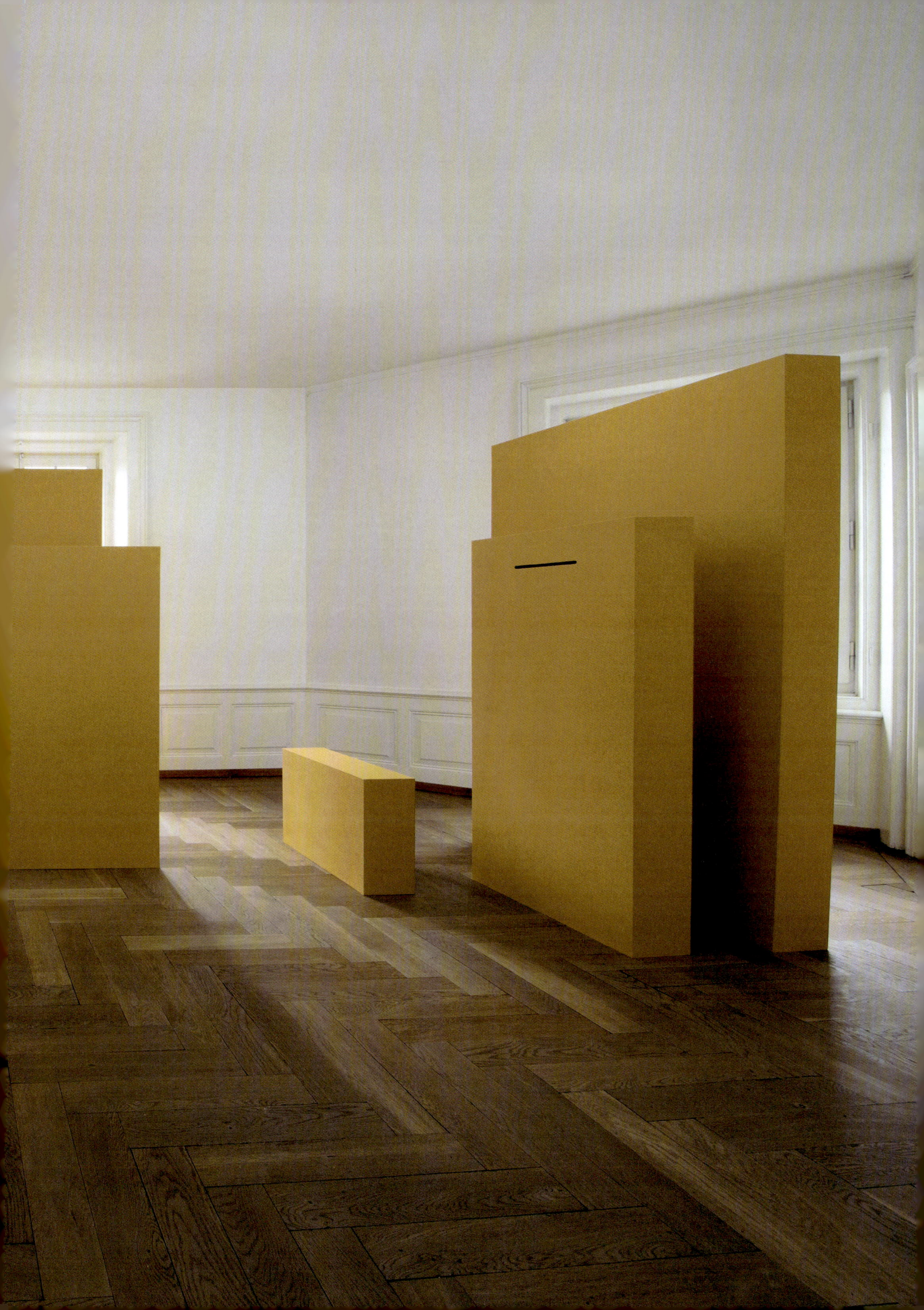

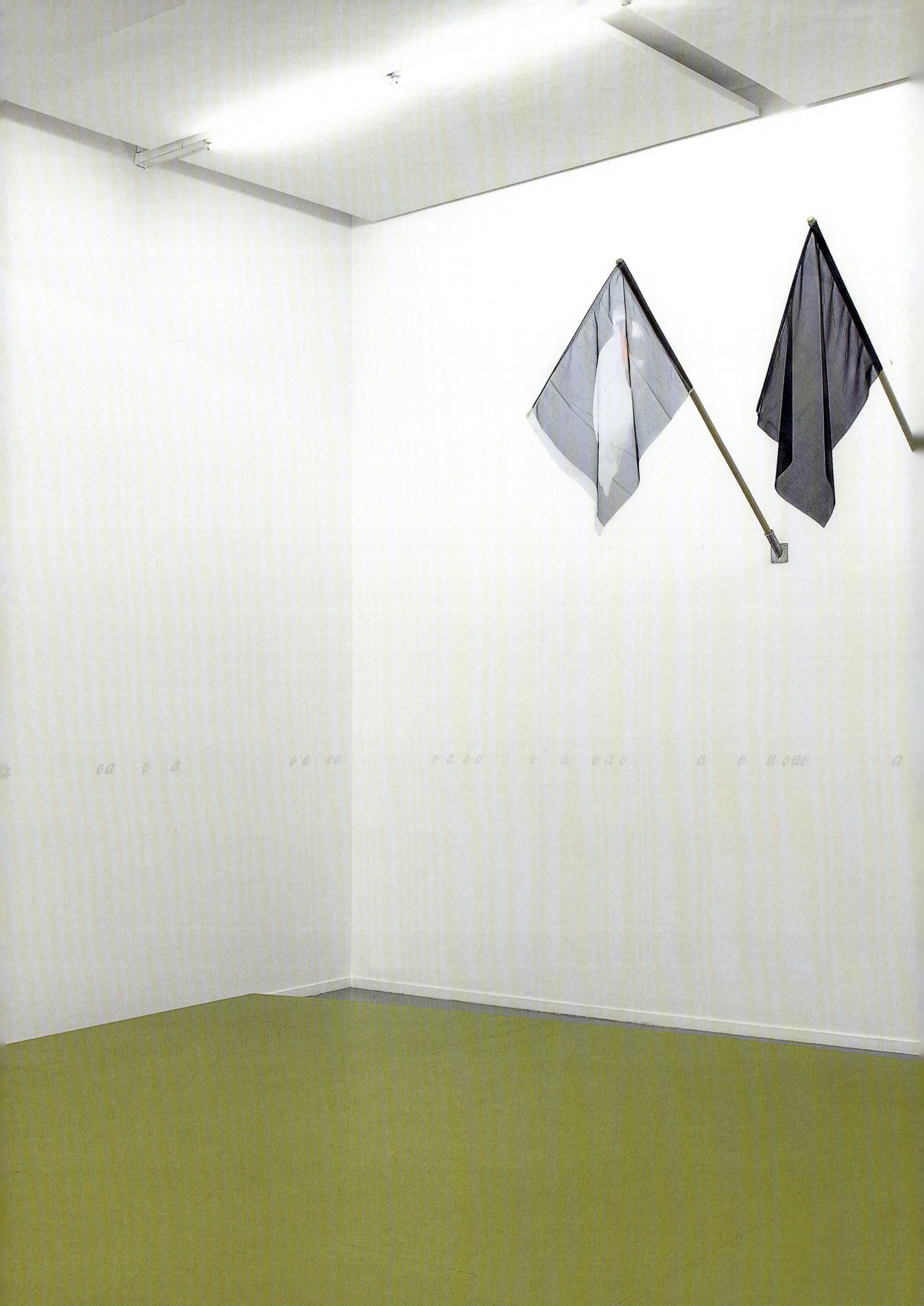

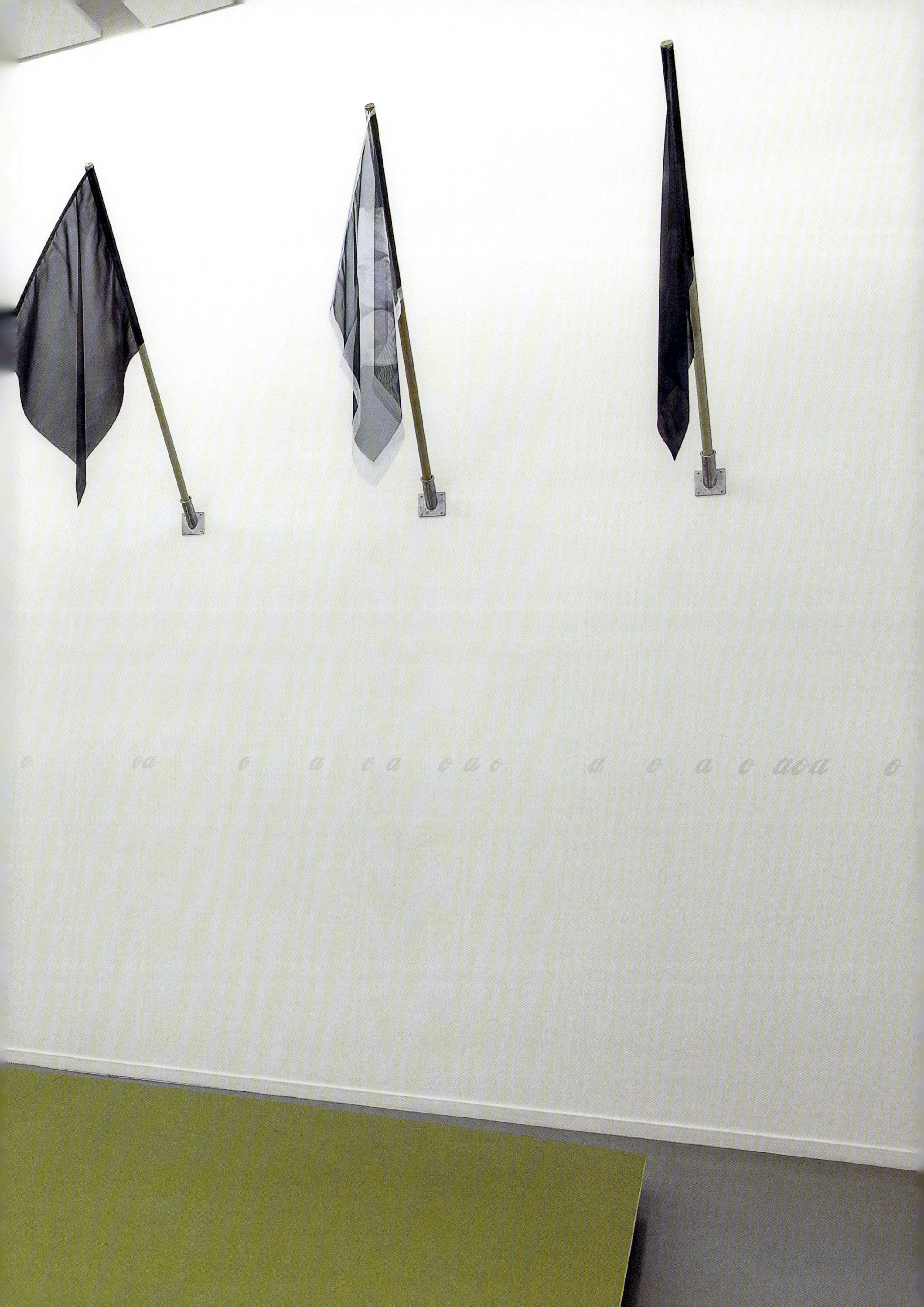
o oa o a oa oao a o a o aoa o

after

authorities

considering

dear

infamous

publicly

sentence

themselves

warning

yourselves

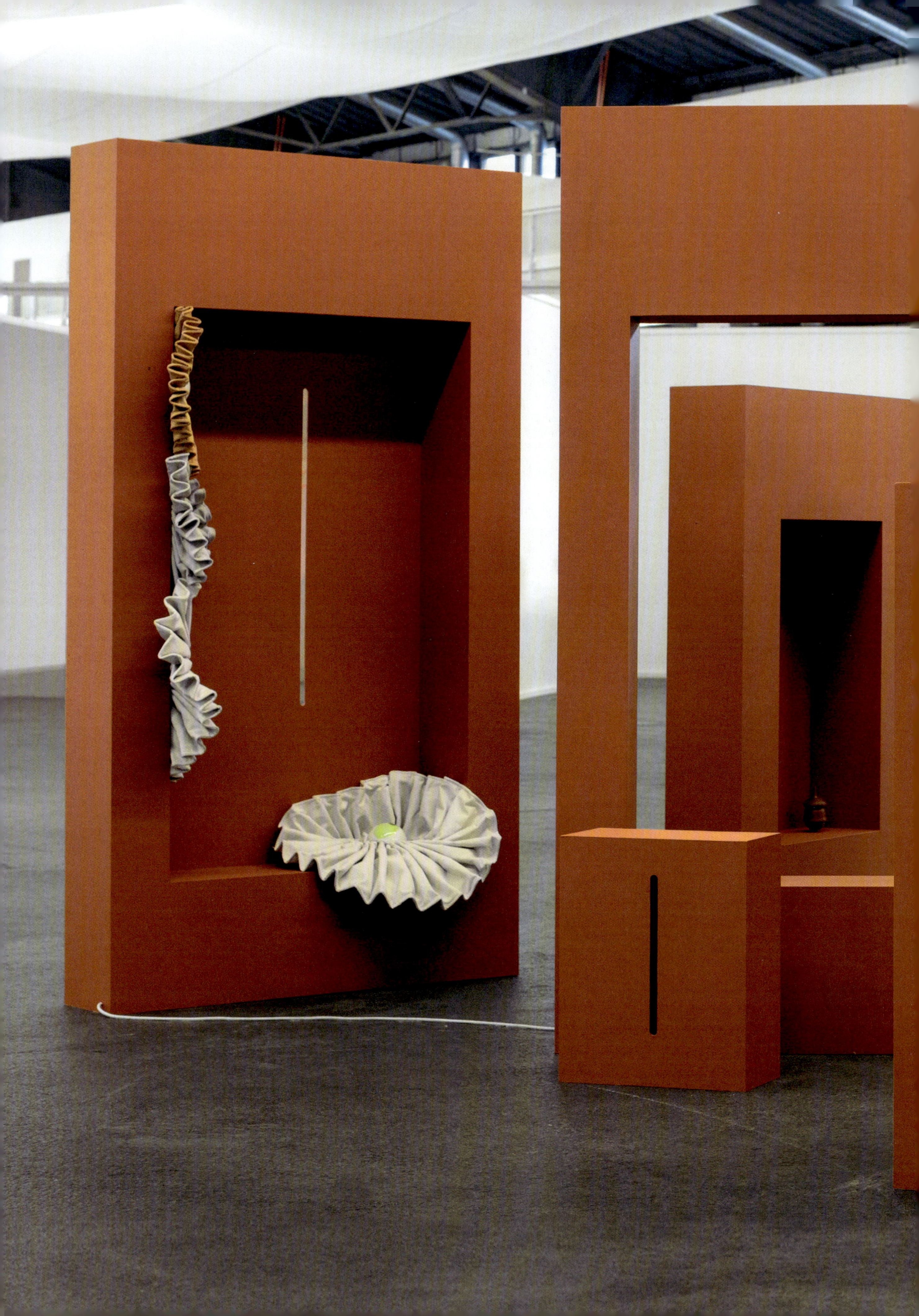

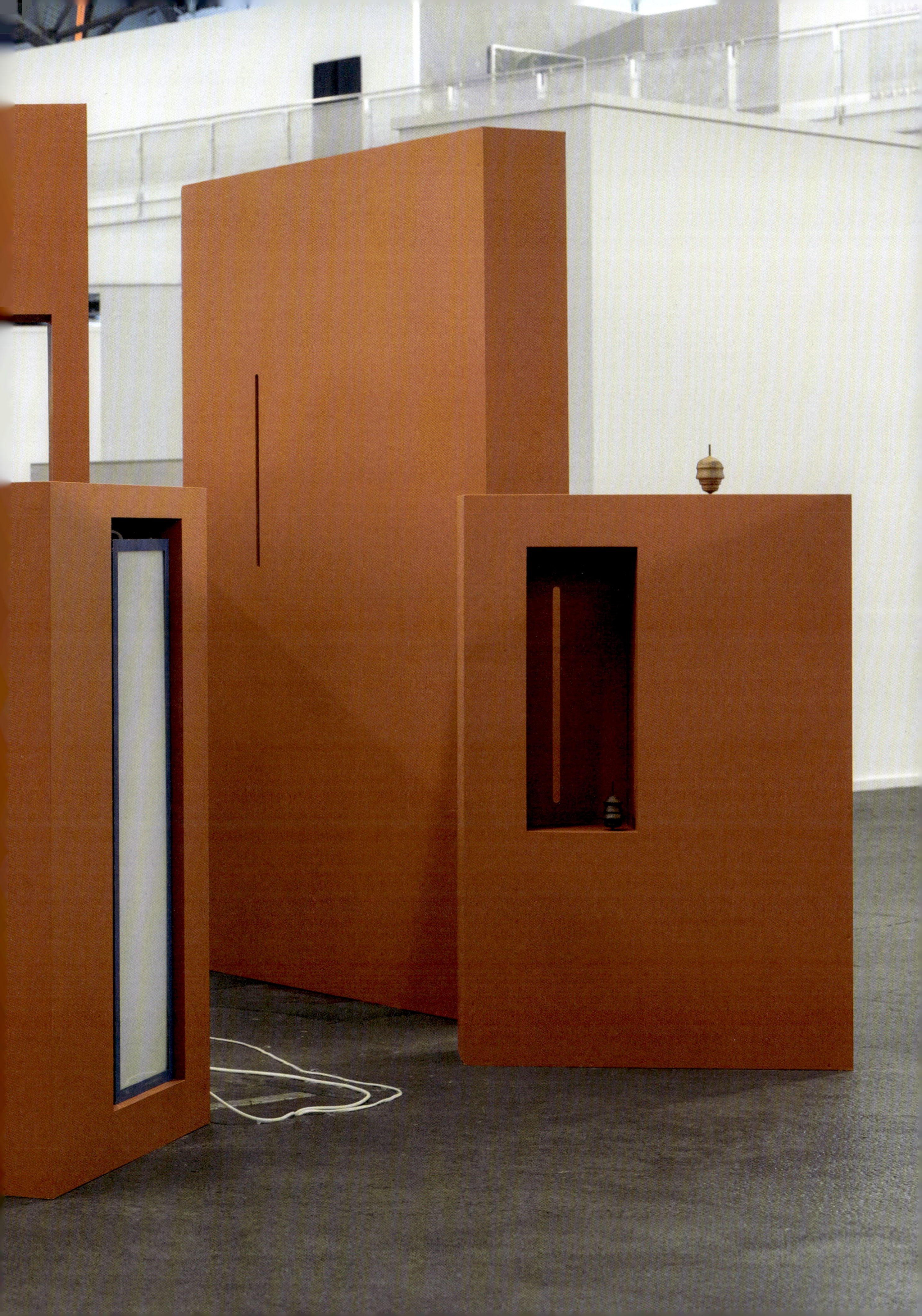

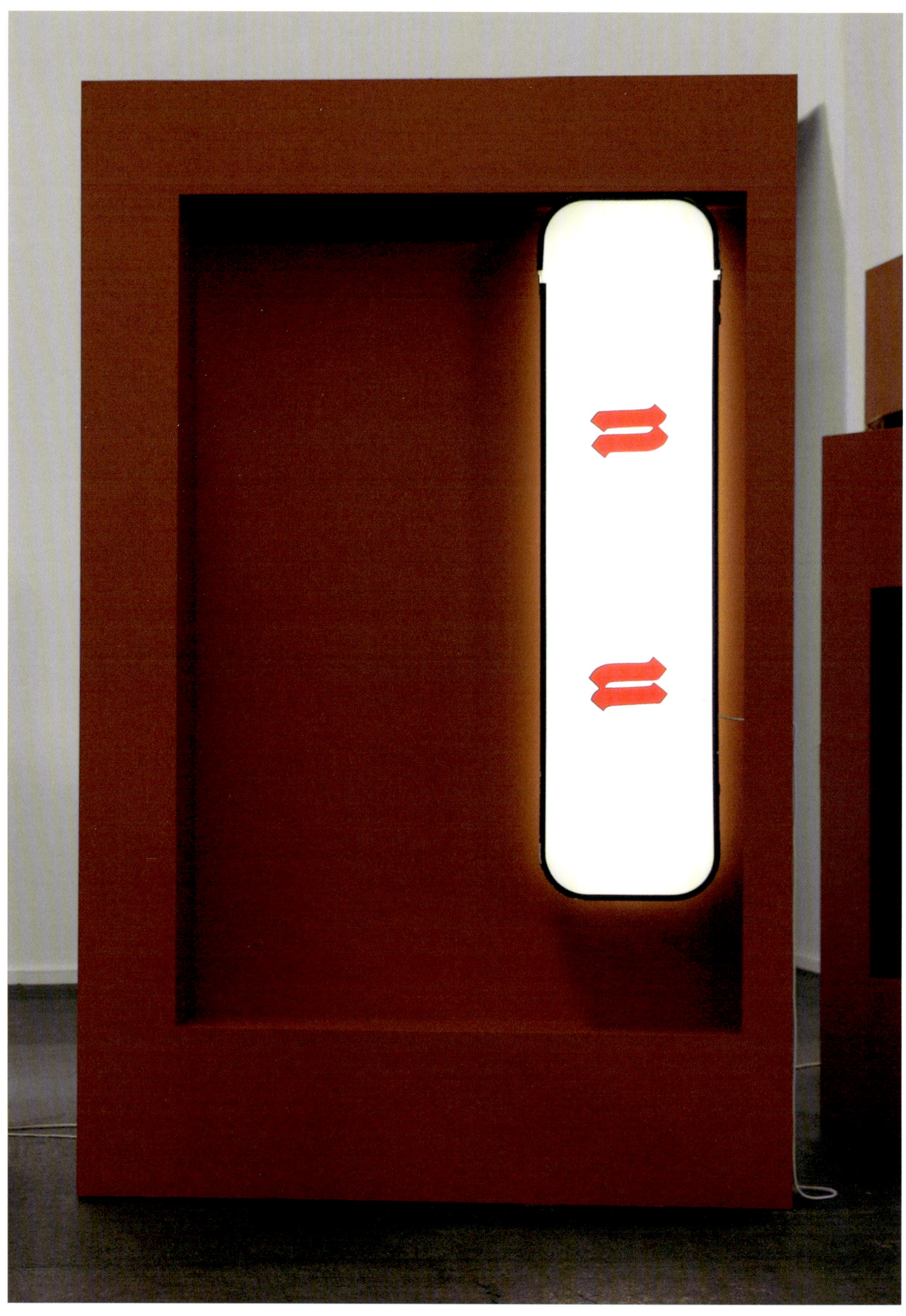

Jalousies modernes, 2021
← *Jalousies modernes*, 2021

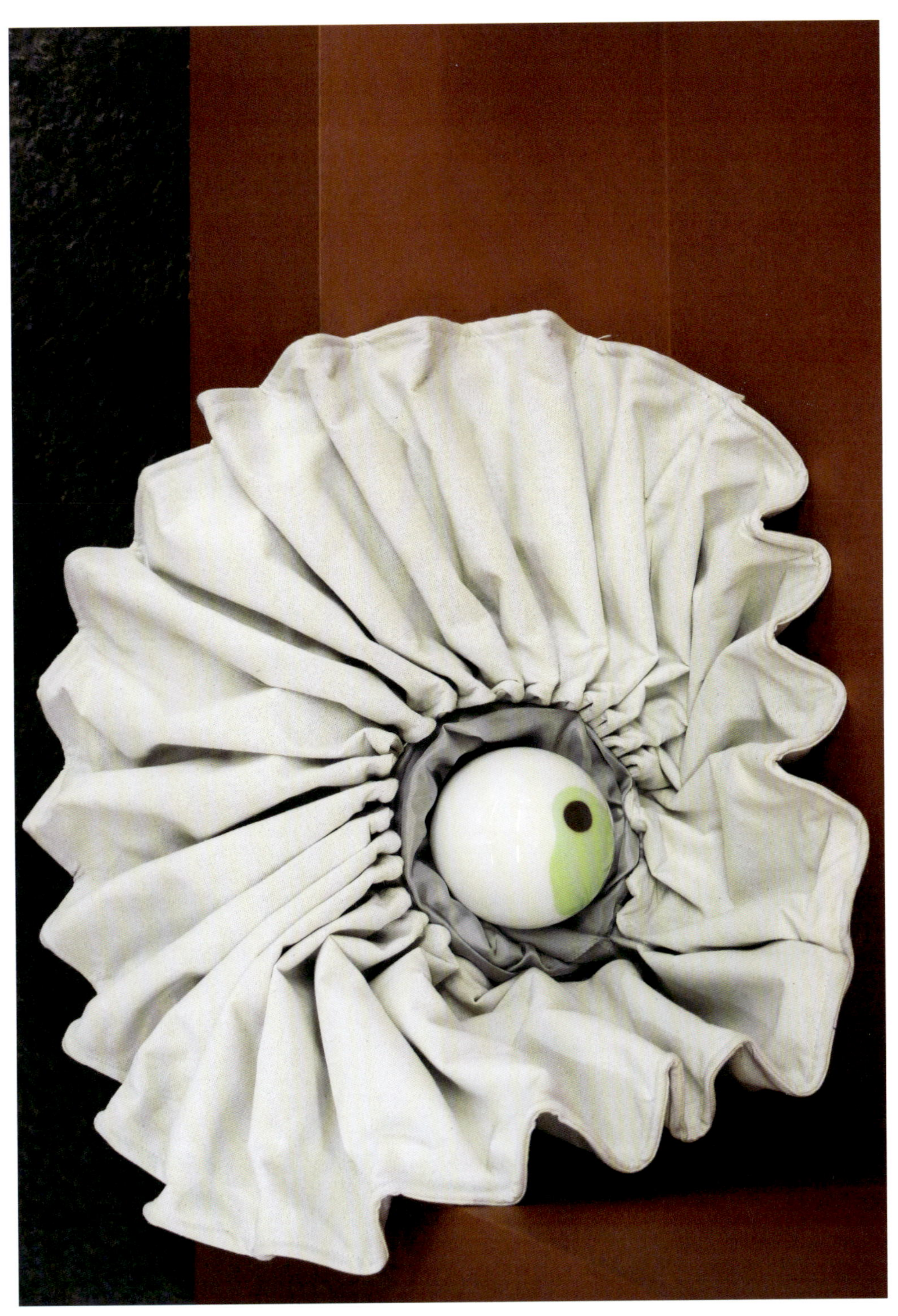

 Jalousies modernes, 2021

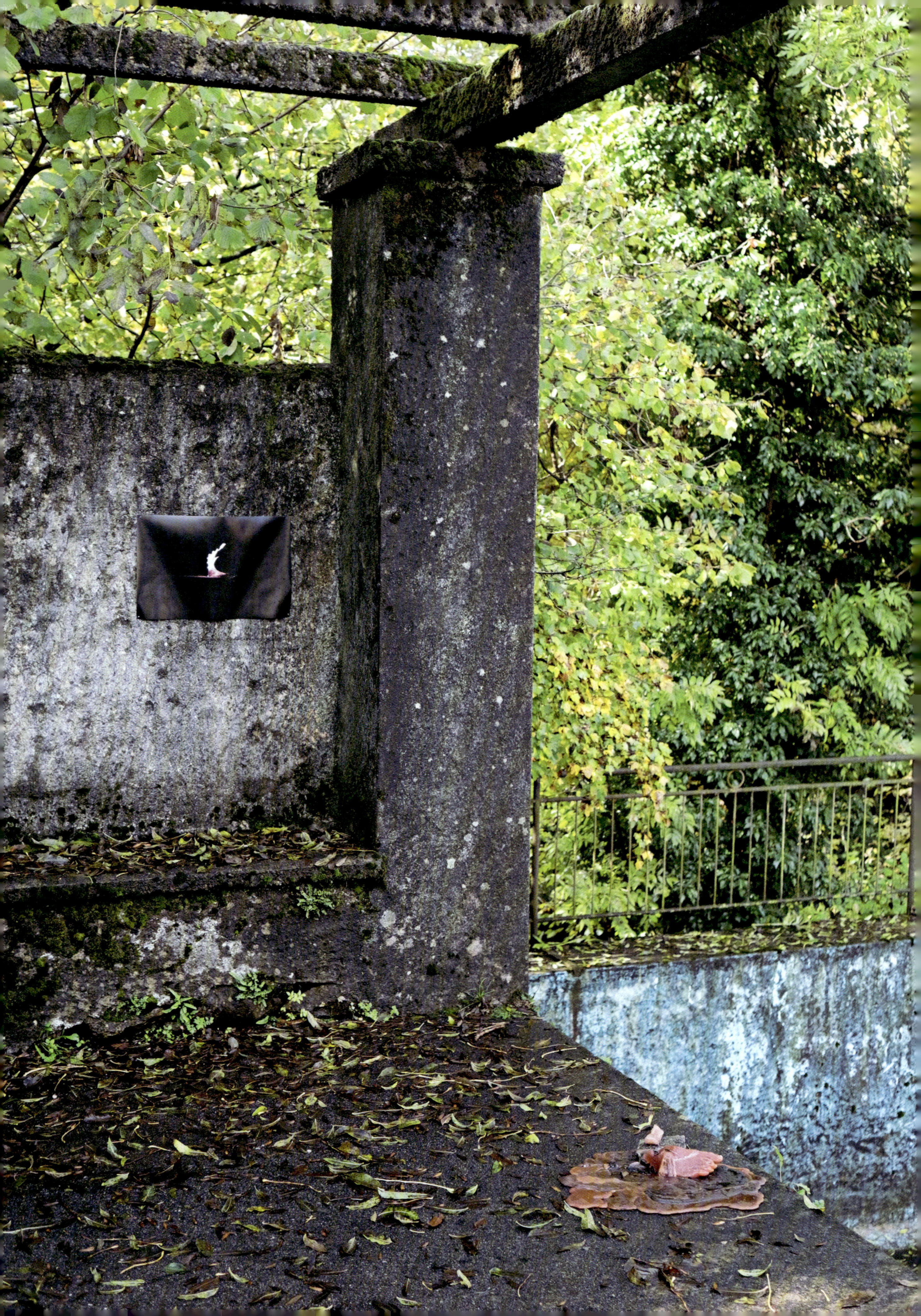

List of Works

p. 2
Fealing Station, 2019
Jump rope, motor, 300 × 350 cm
Exhibition view, *Long Distance Relationship I*, Motrat, Prishtina, 2019

p. 5
Le Rut animal, 2017
Plaster, motorized tongue, c. 50 × 25 × 45 cm
Exhibition view, *Plattform18*, Kunsthaus Langenthal, Langenthal, 2018
Private Collection

p. 6
L'Ami naturel, 2017
Plaster, motorized tongue, c. 50 × 30 × 25 cm
Exhibition view, *Crack a Cold One*, Galerie Derouillon, Paris, 2018
Private Collection

p. 11
Traductrice cleptomane, 2020
Light box, tape, 130 × 18 × 50 cm
Exhibition view, *Agarra-diablo*, CAN–Centre d'art Neuchâtel, Neuchâtel, 2020
Collection Fonds cantonal d'art contemporain, Geneva

p. 12–13
Agarra-diablo, 2020
Partitioned corridor (wood, paint), sandpaper, sand, ball bearing, dimensions variable
Exhibition view, *Agarra-diablo*, CAN–Centre d'art Neuchâtel, Neuchâtel, 2020

p. 14
L'Ami naturel I, 2020
Wood, cotton, satin, motor, soup spoon, 400 × 60 × 20 cm
Produced with Renato Zülli (mechanism)
Exhibition view, *Agarra-diablo*, CAN–Centre d'art Neuchâtel, Neuchâtel, 2020
Collection Musée cantonal des Beaux-Arts de Lausanne, Lausanne

p. 15
Nostalgie en pantoufles (Social Gravity), 2020 (detail)
Wood, tennis ball, paint, lost keys, dimensions variable
Exhibition view, *Agarra-diablo*, CAN–Centre d'art Neuchâtel, Neuchâtel, 2020

p. 16–17
Exhibition view, *Agarra-diablo*, CAN–Centre d'art Neuchâtel, Neuchâtel, 2020

p. 18
L'Ami naturel II, 2020 (detail)
Wood, cotton, satin, motor, soup spoon, 400 × 60 × 20 cm
Produced with Renato Zülli (mechanism)
Exhibition view, *Agarra-diablo*, CAN–Centre d'art Neuchâtel, Neuchâtel, 2020
Collection Musée cantonal des Beaux-Arts de Lausanne, Lausanne

p. 25
Patron/Partner, 2022
Light box, tape, 90 × 22 × 16 cm
Exhibition view, *Moving Jealousy*, Kunst Halle Sankt Gallen, St. Gallen, 2023
Private Collection

p. 26–27
Exhibition view, *Moving Jealousy*, Kunst Halle Sankt Gallen, St. Gallen, 2023

p. 28–29
Can't We Stop Speaking?, 2023
Motorized curtain, video, color, silent, 5'10"
Produced with Claudine Guthmann (curtain)
Exhibition view, *Moving Jealousy*, Kunst Halle Sankt Gallen, St. Gallen, 2023

p. 30
Shadow I, 2023
Fiberglass, cement, veterinary gloves, c. 90 × 50 × 35 cm
Exhibition view, *Moving Jealousy*, Kunst Halle Sankt Gallen, St. Gallen, 2023
Swiss National Bank Collection

p. 31
Shadow II, 2023
Fiberglass, fabric, cement, veterinary gloves, c. 97 × 100 × 52 cm
Exhibition view, *Moving Jealousy*, Kunst Halle Sankt Gallen, St. Gallen, 2023
Swiss National Bank Collection

p. 32
You and/Your Gang, 2023
Wood, brass, wooden beads, mirror, 53 × 62 × 4 cm each
Produced with Stéphane Kropf and Virginie Sistek

Solitary/Solidarity, 2023
Wood, brass, wooden beads, mirror, 68 × 94 cm
Produced with Stéphane Kropf and Virginie Sistek

p. 33
Moving, 2023
Wood, brass, wooden beads, mirror, 40 × 50 cm
Produced with Stéphane Kropf and Virginie Sistek
Private Collection

Solidarity/Solitary, 2023
Wood, brass, wooden beads, mirror, 68 × 94 cm
Produced with Stéphane Kropf and Virginie Sistek
Private Collection

p. 34–35
Dormant Season, 2023
Embroidery with straw, wood, walnut tree, silk paper, paint, 100 × 180 × 7 cm
Produced with Emma Bruschi (straw), Léonie Perret (embroidery) and Stéphane Kropf (frame)
Exhibition view, *Moving Jealousy*, Kunst Halle Sankt Gallen, St. Gallen, 2023
Property of the Swiss Confederation, Bern

p. 36–37
Exhibition view, *Moving Jealousy*, Kunst Halle Sankt Gallen, St. Gallen, 2023

p. 38
Auto-confiance, 2021
Light box and tape, permanent commission for the art space All Stars, Lausanne, 90 × 20 × 9 cm

p. 43
Main courante, 2023 (detail)
Clay, graphite, varnish, brass, steel, dimensions variable
Produced with Bastien Gachet

p. 44–45
Toi et ta bande, 2023
Straw, Plexiglas, nails, 155 × 900 cm
Produced with Emma Bruschi (straw) and Virginie Sistek
Exhibition view, *Jardin d'Hiver #2. Poems of Change*, Musée cantonal des Beaux-Arts de Lausanne, Lausanne, 2023

p. 46–47
Exhibition view, *L'Ami naturel*, Tunnel Tunnel, Lausanne, 2018

p. 48–49
Le Rut animal II, 2018
Plaster, wood, paint, motorized tongue, dimensions variable
Exhibition view, *L'Ami naturel*, Tunnel Tunnel, Lausanne, 2018

p. 50–51
Rassemblées (Suto), 2018
Wood, olfactory paint, sound, dimensions variable
Produced with M. Gharbi (paint)
Exhibition view, *Plattform18*, Kunsthaus Langenthal, Langenthal, 2018

p. 52–53
Passe Passe, 2018
Moving floor, print on mosquito net, sound, dimensions variable
Exhibition view, *Passe Passe*, Centre culturel suisse, Paris, 2018

p. 54–55
Juger les vers, 2023
Video, b&w, silent, 12'
Produced with Pauline Brocart and Quentin Le Garrec
Based on Catherine Chêne, "Juger les vers: exorcismes et procès d'animaux dans le diocèse de Lausanne (XVe-XVIe siècles)," 1995

p. 56–57
Jalousies modernes, 2021
Wood, porcelain, motor, cotton, light box, tape, dimensions variable
Exhibition view, Kiefer Hablitzel Kunstpreis, Basel, 2021

p. 58–59
Jalousies modernes, 2021 (details)
Wood, porcelain, motor, cotton, light box, tape, dimensions variable
Exhibition view, Kiefer Hablitzel Kunstpreis, Basel, 2021

p. 60
L'État des je, 2020
Wax, cotton, c. 25 × 5 × 30 cm
Exhibition view, *It's My Party: Deep End*, Sonnenstube, Lugano, 2020

p. 62–63
Percée parade, 2023
Video, color, silent, 22'54"
Produced with Danilo Gubian (kite) and Anouck Chambaz (film)

p. 64
L'Ombre, 2018–2021
Expanded polystyrene and primer, wood, fabric, rubber, 180 × 130 × 36 cm
Produced with Vox.a
Exhibition view, Locus Solus, Prilly, 2021
Collection Musée d'art du Valais, Sion

Unless indicated otherwise, all works are in the artist's collection.

← *L'État des je*, 2020

Biography

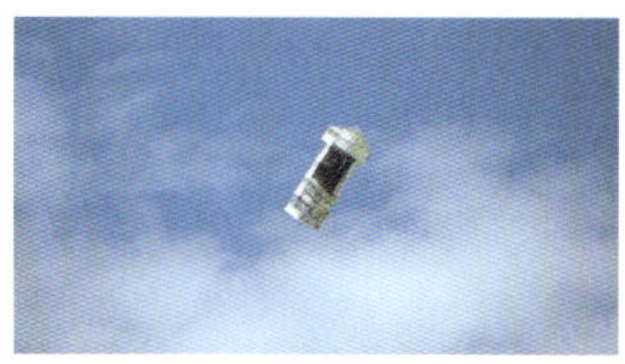

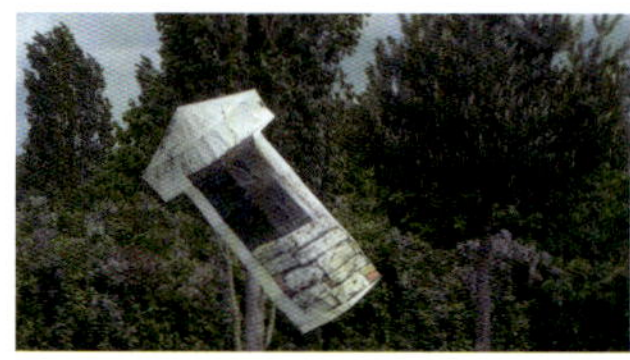

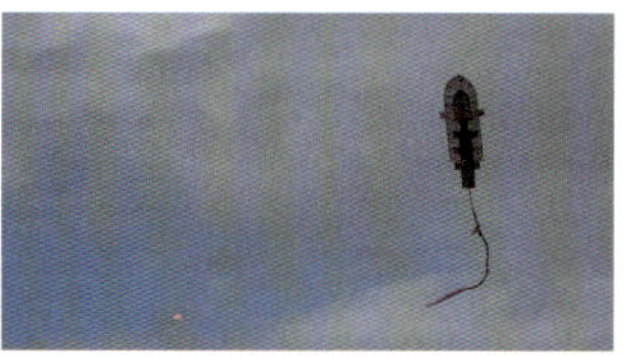

Born in 1994 in Bogotá, Colombia, Gina Proenza lives in Lausanne, Switzerland.

She graduated in Visual Arts from the École Cantonale d'Art de Lausanne (ECAL) in 2017, and also holds a Certificate of Advanced Studies in Dramaturgy and Text Performance from the University of Lausanne and La Manufacture (Haute École des Arts de la Scène). As the co-director at the Forde art space in Geneva (2020–2023) and cofounder of the artist-run-space Pazioli (Renens, 2015–2017), Proenza is actively involved in the arts scene in French-speaking Switzerland. She teaches sculpture and runs a workshop on contemporary writing with Federico Nicolao as part of the Bachelor of Visual Arts at ECAL. Proenza is the winner of the Helvetia Art Prize (2018), the Bourse culturelle de la Fondation Leenaards (2019), the Prix d'art Kiefer Hablitzel (2021), and the Manor Art Prize 2024 Vaud (2024).

SELECTED SOLO EXHIBITIONS

2024
Toi et ta bande, Musée cantonal des Beaux-Arts de Lausanne, Lausanne
Sagas, permanent commission, Cinémathèque suisse, Le Capitole, Lausanne

2023
L'Automne au printemps, Musée des Beaux-Arts, La Chaux-de-Fonds
Moving Jealousy, Kunst Halle Sankt Gallen, St. Gallen

2022
Vestiaires, permanent commission, Urgent Paradise, Lausanne

2021
Locus Solus, Prilly
Dissolving Views, Lemme, Sion
Auto-confiance, permanent commission, All Stars, Lausanne

2020
Agarra-diablo, CAN—Centre d'art Neuchâtel, Neuchâtel

2019
Demain comme hier, with Anaïs Wenger, Point chaud, Lausanne

2018
Passe Passe, Centre culturel suisse, Paris
a a e o, Liste Art Fair, Basel
L'Ami naturel, Tunnel Tunnel, Lausanne

SELECTED GROUP EXHIBITIONS

2023
Desde donde miras el sol?, CAN—Centre d'art Neuchâtel, Neuchâtel
Mirage. La Collection BCV invite Natacha Donzé, Gina Proenza, Jean-Luc Manz et Denis Savary, Musée cantonal des Beaux-Arts de Lausanne, Lausanne
Jardin d'Hiver #2. Poems of Change, Musée cantonal des Beaux-Arts de Lausanne, Lausanne
The Alignement Problem, Live in Your Head, HEAD, Geneva

2022
Prétexte, CALM—Centre d'art La Meute, Lausanne
The Gina Show, City SALTS, Basel

2021
Days Are Where We Live, Art au Centre, Geneva
Môtiers 2021–Art en plein air, Môtiers
Jardin d'Hiver #1. Comment peut-on être (du village d'à côté) persan (martien)?, Musée cantonal des Beaux-Arts de Lausanne, Lausanne

2020
La Totale, Les Moulins, Boissy-le-Châtel
It's My Party: Deep End, Sonnenstube, Lugano

2019
Long Distance Relationship I, Motrat, Pristina
Was erzählt die Romandie?, Galerie Häusler Contemporary, Zurich
Protect Me From What I Want, Kunst Halle Sankt Gallen, St. Gallen
The Big Rip, Bounce Chill Or Crunch?, Last Tango, Zurich

2018
The Way Things Run III, PS120, Berlin
Crack a Cold One, Galerie Derouillon, Paris
La Lampada, Brasserie Atlas, Brussels
Plattform18, Kunsthaus Langenthal, Langenthal

THE WRITERS

Nicolas Brulhart, Director, Kunsthalle Friart, Fribourg

Salome Hohl, Director, Cabaret Voltaire, Zurich

Sabrina Tarasoff, writer and art critic, Paris

Imprint

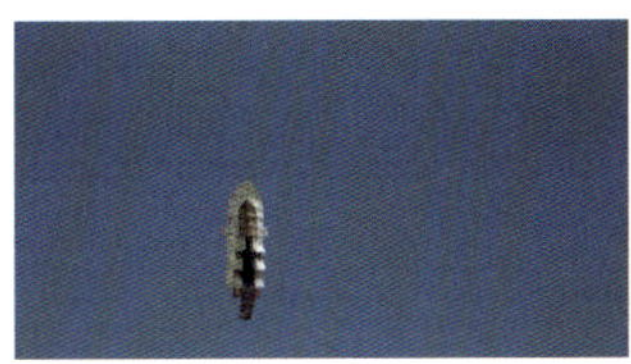

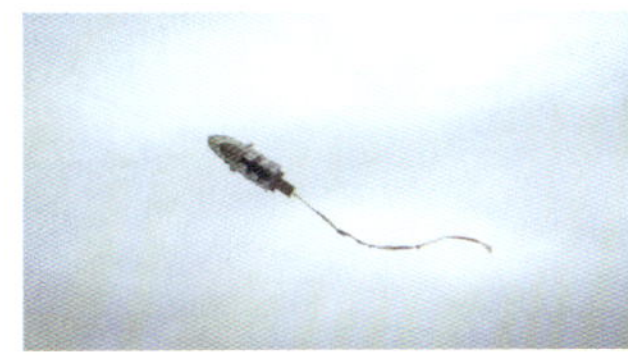

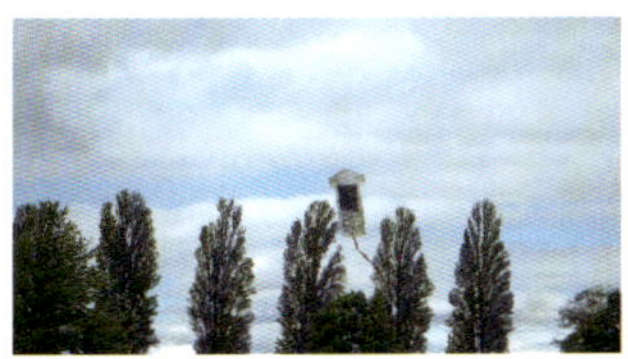

This book is published on the occasion of the exhibition *Gina Proenza. Toi et ta bande*, held at the Musée cantonal des Beaux-Arts de Lausanne from May 24 to September 1, 2024

Exhibition Curator: Nicole Schweizer, Contemporary Art Curator, assisted by Eleonora Del Duca, Assistant Curator

MUSÉE CANTONAL DES BEAUX-ARTS DE LAUSANNE

Director
Juri Steiner

Collection and Exhibitions Department
Catherine Lepdor, Chief Curator

Pierre-Henri Foulon, Camille Lévêque-Claudet, Nicole Schweizer, Curators

Camille de Alencastro, Eleonora Del Duca, Assistant Curators

Françoise Delavy, Stéphanie Ricordeau, Conservators

Marie Beyaert, Sofia Sanfelice di Monteforte, Registrars

Jonas Hänggi, Étienne Malapert, Photographers

Florian Chiaradia, Isabelle Labarthe, Library and Archive Managers

Manuela Giovannini, Archivist

Communication, Marketing, and Press Department
Aline Guberan, Head of Department
Loïse Cuendet, Communication and Digital Projects Advisor
Raphaël Rehm, Graphic Designer
Carole Diserens, Marketing Specialist
Florence Dizdari, Public Relations Specialist, Press Coordinator

Education and Public Experience Department
Sandrine Moeschler, Head of Department
Cécilia Bovet, Gabrielle Chappuis, Gisèle Comte, Staša Genest, Museum Educators

Reception
Anne-Françoise Clerc, Reception Manager
Claudine Bergdolt, Angel von Büren, Reception Agents

Administration and Exploitation Department
Margarida Ramalho, Head of Department

Secretarial Team
Kedsamone McBrayer, Miguel Menezes, Anne Moix

Technical Team
Yassine Gheribi, Head of Department
Mathias a Marca, Édouard Besson, Peter Matthes, Tristan Turchany, Technicians

Security and Surveillance Team
Lucas Beyer, Laurent Burla, and team

Maintenance Team
Patrick Boulaz, Maria Do Carmo Alves Barbeira, Paulo Lemos

Bookshop
Marie-Laure Offredi, Head of Department
Alix Debraine, Romain Follonier, Marie Oliveira, Rafaela Santos

Musée cantonal des Beaux-Arts
Plateforme 10
Place de la Gare 16
CH–1003 Lausanne
www.mcba.ch

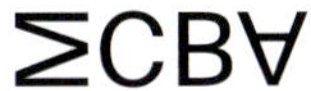

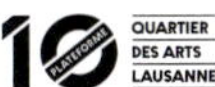

This publication has received the generous support of Manor.

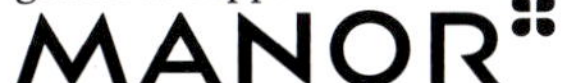

Main Partner

Main Partners for the building of the Musée cantonal des Beaux-Arts de Lausanne:

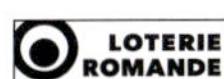

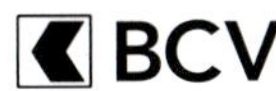

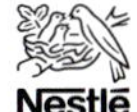

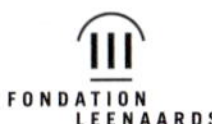

ACKNOWLEDGMENTS

The Musée cantonal des Beaux-Arts de Lausanne would like to thank all the people who made the exhibition and this publication possible: Gina Proenza, the jury of the Manor Art Prize 2024 Vaud (Nicolas Brulhart, Séverine Fromaigeat, Didier Rittener, Pierre-André Maus, Chantal Prod'Hom), Clément Dirié and Nicolas Eigenheer, and the authors of this publication.

Our thanks also go to the whole team at Plateforme 10.

Gina Proenza warmly thanks all the colleagues, friends, lovers, and families who take part in and support her artistic practice as well as the works, doubts, artists, moths, and books that surround it. She would particularly like to thank Nicole Schweizer for her commitment to the exhibition and publication, the entire team at MCBA for their involvement in the exhibition; and Nicolas Brulhart, Salome Hohl, and Sabrina Tarasoff for their invaluable contributions to this publication.

PUBLICATION

Editor
Nicole Schweizer

Editorial Assistance
Eleonora Del Duca

Editorial Coordination
Clément Dirié

Copy Editing and Proofreading
Clare Manchester

Translations
Anna Brailovsky from the German (Hohl), Deke Dusinberre from the French (Schweizer, Conversation)

Graphic Design
Nicolas Eigenheer, with Coline Houot

Typeface
Recital (www.optimo.ch)

Cover
Nu, 2021
Light box, tape, 135 × 16 × 35 cm
Fonds cantonal d'art contemporain Collection, Geneva

Endleaves and illustrations
The leaves and drop initials opening each text are taken from the artist's drawings.

Color Separation and Print
Musumeci S.p.A, Quart (Aosta)

Photo Credits
BAK, Swiss Art Awards/ Guadalupe Ruiz: p. 56–58; Centre culturel suisse/Margot Montigny: p. 52–53 (© ADAGP, Paris, 2024, for Margot Montigny); Collectif Détente: p. 2; Gregory Copitet: p. 6; M. Flury: p. 5, 50–51; Musée cantonal des Beaux-Arts de Lausanne/Jonas Hänggi: p. 38; Musée cantonal des Beaux-Arts de Lausanne/Étienne Malapert: p. 44–45; Musée des beaux-arts de la Chaux-de-Fonds/Gaspard Gigon: p. 43; Mathilda Olmi: p. 46–49; Virginie Otth: p. 64; Gina Proenza: p. 33b, 59; Sebastian Schaub: p. 25–32, 33t, 34–37; Sébastien Verdon: p. 11–18; Sonnenstube/Mattia Angelini: p. 60

Printed in Europe.

PUBLISHED BY

JRP|Editions
Rue des Bains, 39
CH–1205 Geneva
www.jrp-editions.com

With the Musée cantonal des Beaux-Arts de Lausanne

ISBN 978-3-03764-614-4

A French edition is available under the ISBN 978-3-03764-615-1.

JRP|Editions publications are available internationally at selected bookstores and from the following distribution partners:

Switzerland
AVA Verlagsauslieferung AG
www.ava.ch

Germany and Austria
P.S. Publishers' Services
gabriele.kern@publishersservices.de

France
Les presses du réel
www.lespressesdureel.com

UK, European countries, USA, Canada, Asia and Australia
ARTBOOK|D.A.P.
www.artbook.com

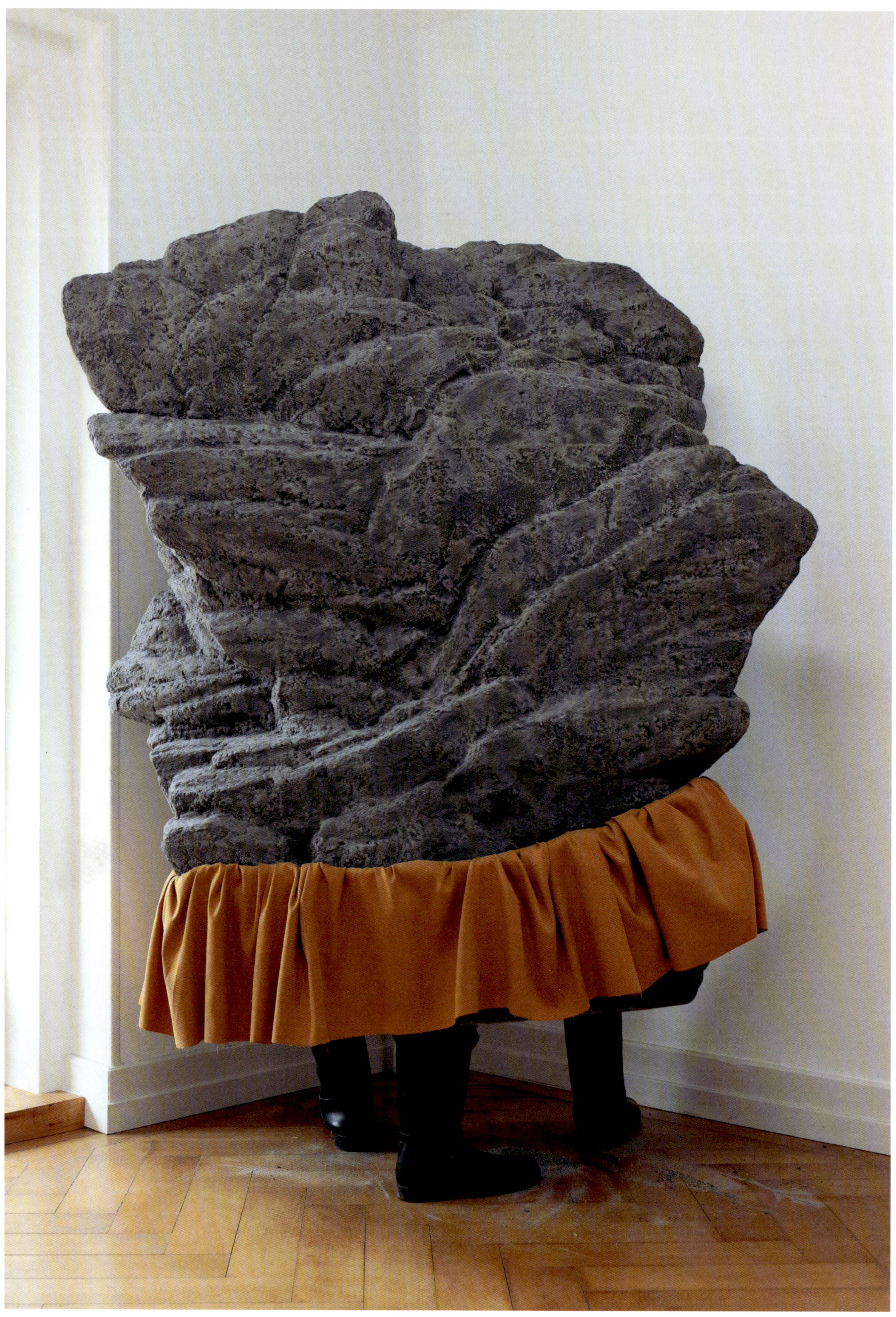

L'Ombre, 2018–2021

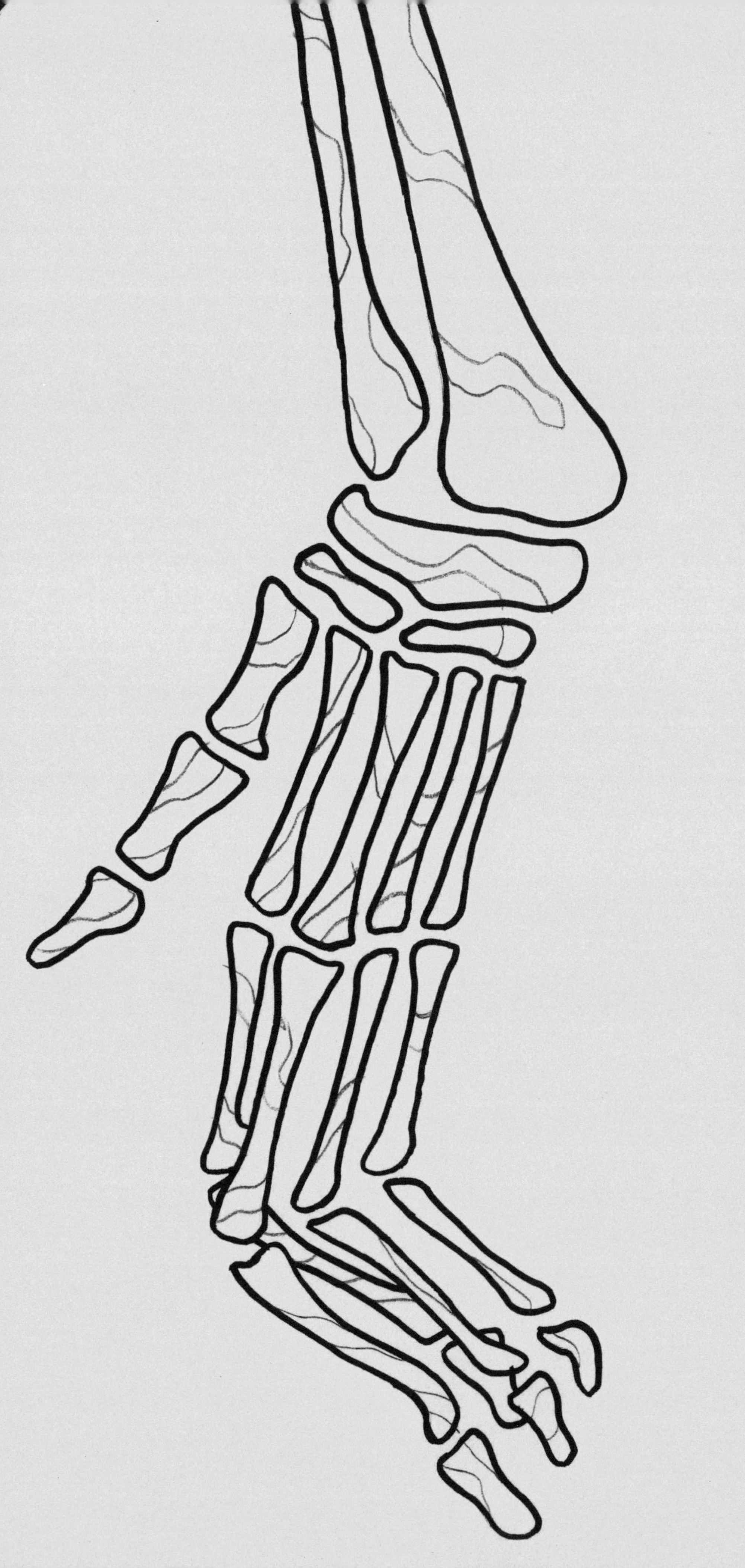